SECRETS OF FAT-FREE CHINESE COOKING

Over 120 low-fat and fat-free, traditional Chinese recipes— from egg rolls to almond cookies

SECRETS OF FAT-FREE CHINESE COOKING

Over 120 low-fat and fat-free, traditional Chinese recipes— from egg rolls to almond cookies

YING CHANG COMPESTINE

Avery Publishing Group
Garden City Park, New York

Text Illustrator: John Wincek
Interior Color Photographer: Victor Giordano
Photo Food Stylist: BC Giordano
Cover Designer: William Gonzalez
Cover Photographer: Victor Giordano
Typesetter: William Gonzalez
In-House Editor: Marie Caratozzolo

The Maximum Daily Fat Intakes table (page 5), the Leanest Beef and Pork Cuts table (page 8), and much of the information on fats and calories presented in Chapter 1 are from *Secrets of Fat-Free Cooking* by Sandra Woodruff, RD (Garden City Park, NY: Avery Publishing Group, 1995).

Library of Congress Cataloging-in-Publication Data

Compestine, Ying Chang.
      Secrets of fat-free Chinese cooking : over 120 fat-free and low-
fat traditional Chinese recipes, from egg rolls to almond cookies /
by Ying Chang Compestine.
            p.   cm.
     Includes index.
     ISBN 0-89529-735-3
      1. Cookery, Chinese. 2. Low-fat diet—Recipes. I. Title.
TX724.5.C5C65   1997
641.5'638—dc21   6-49697
                                       CIP

Printed in the United States of America

10 9 8 7 6 5 4 3 2 1

Contents

To the land I left behind,
and
To the memory of my mother and father.

Acknowledgments

I thank Rudy Shur for providing me with the opportunity to publish this book, and for his professional guidance throughout this project.

Thanks to Marie Caratozzolo. Her knowledge, meticulous scrutiny, and sound judgment strengthened this book. She is the best editor anyone could hope for.

I would also like to thank Karen Hay for her generous efforts in bringing this book to its high state of excellence.

Thanks to Vinson Ming Da Compestine, my son, for giving me the inspiration for this project, and for his endless patience while waiting and watching me cook.

My special thanks goes to my best friend and dear husband, Greg Compestine, for his support, patience, enthusiasm, help, and love.

Foreword

We're all well aware of the importance of proper nutrition in the maintenance of health and the prevention of cardiovascular disease. Unfortunately, the typical American diet is anything but healthy. People love to eat high-fat food because it is readily available and tastes good. Too many people lack experience in preparing low-fat recipes and sadly remain unaware of great dishes that are good for you.

Americanized Chinese food is often high in fat, sodium, and calories, and has been off-limits to those seeking strict limits in fat intake, such as those with coronary heart disease or hypertension. For those of you who are Chinese food lovers as I am, you will welcome *Secrets of Fat-Free Chinese Cooking* as a wonderful breakthrough. Presented to you are numerous recipes of your favorite dishes, prepared using methods and ingredients designed to minimize fat and salt intake and to meet the dietary requirements of the American Heart Association. I personally have tried several of the dishes detailed in this book and have found them to be superb, tasty, and ideal for anyone looking for a means of lowering the fat in their diets.

Whether you have heart disease, hypertension, or are healthy and want to stay that way, I trust you will agree that this book provides a new chance to eat the Chinese dishes you love without sacrificing great taste. Give it a try and your heart will be happy.

Ronald B. Jenkins, M.D.
Director, Boulder Heart Institute
Boulder, Colorado

Introduction

Many of my American friends wonder how I stay slim once they see how much I eat. The answer does not lie in *how much* I eat but in *what* I eat. A nutritional diet based primarily on fresh vegetables, wholesome grains, and moderate amounts of fish and lean meats—all properly prepared—helps keep me physically fit.

Recently, Chinese food has earned a reputation for being unhealthy. It has been associated with deep-frying, high-fat content, and unhealthy levels of salt and MSG.* While this may be characteristic of the food prepared in many Americanized Chinese restaurants, it is far from the case in authentic Chinese dishes, which emphasize the use of fresh ingredients and judicious amounts of meat. The basis of almost every meal is either noodles or rice, and most dishes include foods that are high in carbohydrates and low in fat.

I have a rule of thumb for rating Chinese restaurants. If the menu lacks the names of the dishes in Chinese characters, it is unlikely that the food will be authentic. In many restaurants, however, you can ask to have dishes prepared in an authentic style and without MSG. I have shared this tip with my American friends, and they have reported back to me that this has helped them explore a different type of Chinese cuisine—one that contains more fresh vegetables and less meat and oil.

It is ironic that today, when people in many parts of the world struggle to obtain their basic nutritional needs, one of the greatest health risks in America comes from excessive dietary fat. Excess fat is second only to smoking in its impact on health. Part of the problem stems from an inordinate consumption of meat. Not long after I came to the United States, some friends took me to a steakhouse. The big, thick, tasteless steaks shocked me. In China, four or five meals would be prepared from one of those steaks. While meat is often a featured ingredient in a dish, it is rarely the main one. Rather, meat serves simply to add flavor or color to a dish.

The most common cooking method for Chinese food is stir-frying, which has a reputation for being oily and heavy. The truth is that you can stir-fry in a nonstick wok or frying pan,

---

* Monosodium glutamate (MSG) is the sodium salt of the amino acid glutamic acid, and is commonly used as a flavor enhancer in foods. It causes some individuals to experience dizziness and flushing.

using cooking sprays or small amounts of oil. Where a traditional Chinese cookbook recipe may call for a half cup of oil or more, a similar dish in this book will require at least 90 percent less oil. And while nonstick cooking sprays are pure fat, the amount that comes out in a one-second spray is so small that it adds an insignificant amount of fat to a recipe. In this book, nonstick sprays are used to promote the browning of foods and to prevent foods from sticking to pots and pans. Some recipes in this book call for a small amount of oil in combination with cooking spray. While the spray is for the cooking process, the added oil is for flavoring the dish. This is why I recommend olive oil or sesame oil. You need very little to achieve wonderful flavor.

Delicious meals made from the recipes in this book call for very little or no animal fats or high-cholesterol ingredients. Instead, fresh vegetables, nuts, and soy products, such as low-fat tofu, are used. Although tofu has a reputation in the United States for being bland and tasteless, you will see how it can become flavorful and savory by simply blending it with the right spices and sauces.

Chicken, beef, and pork can be substituted for each other in many of the recipes in this book. I suggest the leanest cuts of meat from organically raised animals.

As the recipes in this book call for flavorful herbs, low-sodium spices, fresh vegetables, and low-fat meats and seafoods, you can feel good about enjoying these dishes without compromising taste. So switch from fat-laden fare to delectable, nutritious meals. Replace cheesecake and ice cream with fresh fruit, and spend a little more time walking, gardening, or hiking instead of watching TV. You will be surprised with how well you will feel!

So, if you:

- love Chinese-style foods. . .

- are interested in trying out new and exciting recipes. . .

- want to try a new approach to a healthy diet. . .

- want to see how food and mind connect. . .

- want to be happy and healthy. . .

it's time to get started!

1. Shopping Guide

Do you believe that Chinese food has to have a high-fat content in order to be flavorful and delicious? Although "Americanized" Chinese restaurants, with their reliance on deep-frying and high-fat ingredients, have helped to earn this reputation, authentic Chinese dishes are actually quite the opposite.

For years, healthful eating has had a reputation of limited choices and deprivation. Most people believed that if food was healthy, it tasted awful. How can plump, juicy dumplings, flavorful rice and noodle dishes, and savory Oriental-style entrées be both delicious and healthy? *Secrets of Fat-Free Chinese Cooking* introduces you to a variety of innovative low-fat and fat-free cooking techniques, and shows you how to turn simple traditional ingredients into authentic Chinese favorites. These dishes are delicious, simple to prepare, and sure to please even those with the most discriminating tastes.

This chapter begins with information on the importance of reducing your dietary fat, and then presents guidelines for budgeting your daily fat intake. A glossary of the best ingredients to use in your low- and no-fat Chinese dishes follows.

A Word About Nutrition

Why is it so important to pay attention to your fat intake? Reducing dietary fat is critical to your optimal health and well-being. The information in the following section explains why.

IMPORTANCE OF FIGHTING FAT

Among the many good reasons to fight fat, the desire to lose weight is probably the most common. How does fighting fat help with weight loss? With more than twice the calories of carbohydrates or protein, fat is a concentrated source of calories. Compare a cup of corn oil (pure fat) with a cup of flour (almost pure carbohydrates). The oil has over 1,900 calories and the flour has 400 calories. It's easy to see where most of our calories come from.

In addition to being high in calories, fat is also readily converted into body fat when eaten in excess. Carbohydrate-rich foods eaten in excess are also stored as fat, but must first be converted into fat—a process that burns up some of the carbohydrates. The bottom line is that a high-fat diet will cause 20 percent more weight gain than will a high-carbohydrate diet, even when the two diets contain the same number of calories. So a high-fat diet is double trouble for the weight-conscious person. It is high in calories, and it is the kind of nutrient that is most readily stored as body fat.

High-fat diets also pose a threat to much more than our weight. Fatty diets can lead to obesity, and result in diseases like diabetes and high blood pressure. And specific types of fat present their own unique problems. For example, eating too much saturated fat—found in meat, butter, and margarine, among other foods—raises blood cholesterol levels, and increases the chances of heart disease. Polyunsaturated fat, once thought to be the solution to heart disease, can also be harmful when eaten in excess. A diet overly rich in certain vegetable oils—corn, sunflower, and safflower, and products made from these oils—is implicated in the development of blood clots, high blood pressure, and inflammatory diseases. Too much polyunsaturated fat can also promote free-radical damage to cells, contributing to heart disease and cancer.

What about monounsaturated fats? Abundant in olive oil, canola oil, avocados, cashews, almonds, and peanuts, monounsaturated fats have no known harmful effects other than being a concentrated source of calories, like all fats.

One other kind of fat needs to be considered—especially if you are concerned about heart disease. Trans-fatty acids, also called trans fats, are chemically altered fats that are produced by adding hydrogen to liquid vegetable oils. This hydrogenation process transforms the liquid vegetable oils into solid margarines and shortenings, giving these products a butter-like consistency. While hydrogenation improves the cooking and baking qualities of oils, and extends their shelf life as well, it also creates trans fats. And trans fats,

it has been found, act much like saturated fats to raise levels of LDL, or "bad" cholesterol, and at the same time lower levels of HDL, or "good" cholesterol.

With all of the problems caused by excess fat, you may think it would be best to completely eliminate fat from your diet. But the fact is that some dietary fat is necessary. For instance, linoleic acid, a polyunsaturated fat naturally abundant in oils such as corn, soy, and safflower, and in walnuts, pine nuts, sunflower seeds, and sesame seeds, is essential for life. The average adult needs a minimum of 3 to 6 grams of linoleic acid per day—the amount present in one to two teaspoonfuls of polyunsaturated vegetable oil or one to two tablespoonfuls of nuts or seeds. Linolenic acid, a fat present mainly in fish, flaxseeds, and green plants, is also essential for good health. Some fat is also needed in the diet so that we may absorb fat-soluble nutrients like vitamin E.

The problem is that many people are getting too much of a good thing. The liberal use of mayonnaise, oily salad dressings, margarine, and cooking oils has created an unhealthy overdose of linoleic acid in the American diet. And, of course, most people also eat far too much saturated fat. The best way to correct this is to minimize the use of refined vegetable oils and table fats, and eat a diet rich in whole grains, legumes, vegetables, and fruits, with moderate amounts of nuts and seeds, fish, and, if desired, lean meats.

WAYS TO FIGHT FAT

Understanding some of the reasons you should get the fat out of your diet is the first step in fighting fat. The following pages will teach you how to develop your own personal fat budget. You will become acquainted with the healthful foods that can help you prune the fat from your diet and maximize the nutrients. The balance of this book shows you how to use these foods to create delicious Chinese fare that you will be proud to serve, and family and friends will love to eat.

Budgeting Fat

About 40 percent of the calories in the average American diet comes from fat. However, currently it is recommended that fat calories constitute no more than 30 percent of the diet, and, in fact, 20 to 25 percent would be even better in most cases. So the amount of fat you should eat every day is based on the number of calories you need. Because people's calorie needs depend on their weight, age, gender, activity level, and metabolic rate, these needs vary greatly among people. Most adults, though, must consume 13 to 15 calories per pound to maintain their weight. Of course, some people need even fewer calories, while very physically active people need more.

Once you have determined your calorie requirements, you can estimate a fat budget for yourself. Suppose you are a moderately active person who weighs 150 pounds. You will probably need about 15 calories per pound to maintain your weight, or about 2,250 calories per day. To limit your fat intake to 20 percent of your caloric intake, you can eat no more than 450 calories derived from fat per day (2,250 x .20 = 450). To convert this to grams of fat, divide by 9, as one gram of fat has 9 calories. Therefore, you should limit yourself to 50 grams of fat per day (450 ÷ 9 = 50).

The table presented below shows two recommended maximum daily fat-gram budgets—one based on 20 percent of calorie intake, and one based on 25 percent of calorie intake. If you are overweight, go by the weight you would like to be. This will allow you to gradually reach your goal weight. And keep in

Maximum Daily Fat Intakes

Weight	Recommended Daily Calorie Intake (13–15 calories per pound)	Fat Grams Allowed (20% of Calorie Intake)	Fat Grams Allowed (25% of Calorie Intake)
100	1,300–1,500	29–33	36–42
110	1,430–1,650	32–37	40–46
120	1,560–1,800	34–40	43–50
130	1,690–1,950	38–43	47–54
140	1,820–2,100	40–46	51–58
150	1,950–2,250	43–50	54–62
160	2,080–2,400	46–53	58–67
170	2,210–2,550	49–57	61–71
180	2,340–2,700	52–60	65–75
190	2,470–2,850	55–63	69–79
200	2,600–3,000	58–66	72–83

Maximum Daily Fat Intakes chart, as well as much of the information on fats and calories, has been reprinted from *Secrets of Fat-Free Cooking* by Sandra Woodruff, R.D. (Garden City Park, NY: Avery Publishing Group, 1995).

mind that although you have budgeted X amount of fat grams per day, you don't have to eat that amount of fat—you just have to avoid going over budget.

Don't Go Too Low

To maximize your health, if you are like most people, you must reduce your daily fat intake. How low should you go? Remember, some fat is necessary for good health. Therefore, you should not try to consume less than 20 grams of fat per day. Of course, if you eat a balanced diet rich in whole, natural foods, it would be almost impossible to eat less than this, anyway. On the other hand, if you eat a diet rich in fat-free refined and processed foods, you could be at risk for a deficiency of essential fats, as well as deficiencies of other nutrients. The authentic Chinese-style recipes in this book include whole grains and other natural foods, and minimize the use of refined and processed ingredients.

If you have a specific medical problem, be sure to check with your physician or nutritionist before making any dramatic dietary changes. Be aware that a very low-fat diet is not for everyone.

Don't Forget About Calories

As discussed earlier, weight loss is the number-one reason that most people are trying to reduce their fat intake. And over the past decade, Americans have been able to reduce their fat consumption from 40 percent of calories to about 34 percent. Yet during this same time, the rate of obesity has actually increased. Now, one out of three Americans is considered obese—compared with one out of four in 1980. The problem is that people tend to forget that calories count too. The fact is that people now eat more calories than they did a decade ago—and exercise less.

The recent avalanche of fat-free products has actually contributed to our nation's "weight" problem. Many people mistakenly think that if a food is low in fat or fat-free, they can consume unlimited quantities of it. For instance, they may start their day with a jumbo bagel with fat-free cream cheese, snack on low-fat cookies and crackers, and eat a few scoops of fat-free ice cream after dinner. Although all of these foods are better choices than their full-fat counterparts, they are loaded with sugar and provide few or no nutrients. And some of these products have just as many calories as the full-fat versions. The truth is that any food eaten in excess of calories burned in a day will be converted to body fat. And this is just as true of fat-free foods as it is of high-fat ones.

This does not mean that you should forget about using fat-free foods to lose weight. These foods, when consumed wisely, can help you reach and maintain a healthy body weight. Setting up a fat budget is the best place to start, since a low-fat diet is generally low in calories, too—unless you eat too many fat-free junk foods. If you then stay within the limits of your fat budget and choose mostly nutrient-rich foods, you should be able to reach your weight-management goals. But if you find that you are still having trouble losing or maintaining weight, you must consider whether you are staying within the bounds of your calorie budget, as well.

Choosing the Best Ingredients

Today, it is not necessary to travel to a Chinatown district to find special ingredients. Many American grocery stores now carry a variety of Chinese-style ingredients and spices. (On the other hand, you can always expect to find better prices in an authentic Chinese grocery, especially on bulk purchases of items such as rice and noodles.) Don't be shy about asking your grocery-store manager to special order an item for you. Most likely, he or she will be happy to oblige.

Authentic Chinese-style cooking is naturally healthful. The use of a variety of fresh vegetables, healthful grains, and flavorful spices translates into nutritious, delectable fare. I have always had a long-time love for anything fresh. When I cook, fresh ingredients always take precedence over others. Fresh vegetables, herbs, and spices bring a wonderful taste to dishes. I use powdered spices such as ginger and garlic only in an emergency; to me, these processed substitutes are too far removed from the world around us. I love to smell the freshness of a just-cut green onion or crisp bell pepper, especially when it has come from my own garden. This shows a full connection with the Earth and the life that is all around us.

Most traditional Chinese cookbooks require a variety of special and unusual ingredients that may overwhelm even the most experienced cooks. This book, on the other hand, calls for ingredients that are easily found in all Asian markets, most health food stores, and many American grocery stores.

Most canned or bottled items can be kept indefinitely when stored in a cool, dry place. Once opened, many of these items must be resealed and possibly refrigerated (be sure to check labels). Most dry herbs and spices can be kept in the pantry, although storing such items in the freezer best preserves their flavor.

Let's take a look at some of the ingredients used throughout this book to ensure delicious low- and no-fat authentic Chinese dishes.

MEATS AND POULTRY

Due to the high fat and cholesterol contents of meats, many people have either sharply reduced their consumption of meat, limited themselves to white meat chicken or turkey, or totally eliminated meat and poultry from their diets. The good news is that authentic Chinese meals call for only small amounts of meat or poultry, which are usually added to provide a hint of flavor or a splash of contrasting color to a dish. What's more, plenty of lean meats and poultry are now available.

Chicken

Chicken, which is a good source of protein, is lower in fat than most cuts of beef and pork, and therefore is a valuable ingredient in low-fat cooking. However, be aware that chicken skin contains high amounts of saturated fat and should be removed before cooking. Many cuts of chicken, if eaten with the skin on, contain more fat than some cuts of beef and pork. As the white meat contains less fat than the dark, I avoid using leg and thigh portions. I prefer using organic chicken breast fillets.

To prevent bacterial growth, always keep uncooked chicken in the refrigerator until you are ready to cook it. For this same reason, it is best to defrost frozen chicken overnight in the refrigerator, not on the kitchen counter. Be sure to wash the chicken carefully before preparing it. When cutting chicken or any meat, always wash the knife and the cutting surface with soap and hot water to prevent bacterial contamination.

Beef and Pork

Although beef and pork are not as lean as poultry, they are both considerably leaner today than in the past. Competition from the poultry industry has caused many beef and pork producers to change breeding and feeding practices, resulting in the reduced-fat content of these products. Even butchers are now trimming away more of the fat from retail cuts of meat, resulting in leaner products. On the average, grocery store cuts of beef are 27 percent leaner today than in the early 1980s, and retail cuts of pork are 43 percent leaner.

Always buy fresh beef and pork. Traditional Chinese dishes require relatively small amounts. I prefer to buy very lean, hormone-free beef and pork from a reputable butcher or grocer. When buying beef, I prefer eye of round, top round, and tip round, which are the lowest in fat and easy to slice and shred. When selecting pork, I prefer the tenderloin, chops, or a good cut of rump purchased from a butcher. If you buy packaged pork from a grocery store, don't choose cuts that have an excessive amount of liquid in the package or are dull in color. Look for pork that has a good pink color.

The following table will guide you in selecting beef and pork cuts that are lowest in fat.

The Leanest Beef and Pork Cuts

Cut (3 ounces, cooked and trimmed)	Calories	Fat
Beef		
Eye of Round	143	4.2 grams
Top Round	153	4.2 grams
Round Tip	157	5.9 grams
Top Sirloin	165	6.1 grams
Pork		
Tenderloin	139	4.1 grams
Boneless Sirloin Chops	164	5.7 grams
Boneless Loin Roast	165	6.1 grams
Boneless Loin Chops	173	6.6 grams

Identifying the lowest-fat cuts of meat is an important first step in healthy cooking, but be aware that even lean cuts have varying amounts of fat because of grade differences. In general, the more expensive USDA Prime and Choice grades of meat contain more fat, much of which is marbelized within the meat and cannot be trimmed away. USDA Select meats have the least amount of marbling, and, therefore, the lowest amount of fat. These differences are significant—a USDA Choice piece of meat may have 15 to 20 percent more fat than a USDA Select cut, and USDA

Prime may have even more fat. There is an obvious and significant difference.

Before cooking pork or beef, always trim off any visible fat. And remember that cutting meat against the grain helps to break up the long fibers, making the meat tender.

Ground Meats

When shopping for ground meats (as well as other cuts) I always choose the leanest varieties. I also prefer hormone-free meats. Ground turkey breast, which is only 1 percent fat by weight, is the leanest ground meat you can find. Ground dark meat turkey made without the skin is 8 to 10 percent fat by weight, and brands with added skin and fat usually contain at much as 15 percent fat. Ground chicken, like ground turkey, often contains skin and fat. Most brands contain at least 15 percent fat. So be sure to read labels carefully before you buy.

Low-fat ground beef is also available. The leanest ground beef commonly sold in supermarkets is 95-percent lean. How different is the leaner ground beef from the more commonly sold product? A 3-ounce cooked serving of 95-percent lean beef contains 132 calories and 4.9 grams of fat. The same size serving of regular beef (73-percent lean) has 248 calories and 17.9 grams of fat. Your fat and calorie savings are obvious.

The leaner gound-meat varieties are generally more expensive. But keep in mind that less fat means less will cook away, so dollar-for-dollar, you will actually be getting more for your money.

FISH AND SEAFOOD

Some fish, such as sole, halibut, and cod are almost fat-free, while others are moderately fatty. However, the oil that fish provide contains omega-3 fatty acids—an essential substance that most people do not eat in sufficient quantities. Valuable omega-3 fatty acids can help reduce blood cholesterol, lower blood

Preparing Meats

Small amounts of thinly sliced strips of meat serve to add flavor and color to Chinese-style dishes. I often prepare enough meat in advance to use in several meals.

1. To prepare the marinade, combine the cornstarch, water, soy sauce, wine, and oil in a medium bowl, and stir until the cornstarch has dissolved. Add the garlic, ginger, and sesame shake. Set aside.

2. To make the meat easier to slice, let it harden a little in the freezer for about 30 minutes. Slice the chilled meat against the grain into thin 1-inch strips. Place the strips in the marinade, toss to coat, and refrigerate at least 1 hour or overnight.

3. Lightly coat a nonstick wok or frying pan with cooking spray. Add the canola oil and place over medium-high heat. When the oil is hot, add the marinated strips and stir-fry for 1 to 2 minutes. Add 2 tablespoons of water and cook another minute.

4. Transfer the cooked strips to an airtight container and refrigerate. The meat will stay fresh for three or four days and can be used in several meals.

8 ounces pork, beef, or chicken breast fillets

1 teaspoon canola oil

MARINADE

2 teaspoons cornstarch

2 tablespoons water

2 tablespoons low-sodium soy sauce

1 1/2 teaspoons cooking wine

1 teaspoon sesame oil

4 cloves garlic, minced

1 tablespoon minced fresh ginger

1/2 teaspoon Eden Foods sesame shake, or 1/4 teaspoon Mrs. Dash seasoning

---

pressure, and prevent the formation of dangerous blood clots. This means that all kinds of fish are considered healthful, even the higher-fat varieties.

In their natural habitat, fish feed on plankton and smaller fish. Many fish, however, are now raised on "farms" where they are fed a diet of grains. As a result, farm-raised fish contain as much or more fat than wild fish do, and they are much lower in the beneficial omega-3 fatty acids.

Many people are concerned with the cholesterol content of shellfish. However, with the exception of shrimp, a 3-ounce serving of most shellfish contains about 60 milligrams of cholesterol. (The maximum recommended limit is 300 milligrams per day.) An equivalent serving of shrimp has about 160 milligrams of

cholesterol. All seafood, including shellfish, is very low in saturated fat. And saturated fat has a greater cholesterol-raising effect than does cholesterol.

Fish is highly perishable, so it is important to know how to select a high-quality product. When I shop for fresh whole fish, I always look for ones with clear eyes, red gills, and shiny skin. This indicates that the fish is fresh and tasty. When buying fish fillets, I make sure that the flesh is firm and has a clean seaweed odor, rather than a "fishy" smell.

Much of the shrimp sold in the United States has been flash-frozen. Fresh shrimp that has been flash-frozen can be delicious when handled and stored properly. Frozen shrimp that is pink in color means that it has already been cooked and has lost most of its flavor. Look for those that are gray or white. Also, when purchasing packages of frozen shrimp, inspect the shells for signs of freezer burn. Some shrimp, depending on the species, harvest location, and time of harvest, may have a slight iodine flavor. This does not indicate spoilage. Spoiled shrimp have an ammonia-like smell.

VEGETABLES

I love fresh vegetables and always have two or three varieties on hand at any given time. When shopping for vegetables, be careful not to buy too much at once; most are quite perishable and may not keep for more than a few days. Although there is nothing like fresh, I always keep a few bags of mixed vegetables stored in the freezer. They often provide a last-minute spark of color and nutrition to a dish.

Some of the vegetables used throughout this book are described below. Most are available at your local grocery store.

Anaheim peppers. *See* Chili peppers.

Bamboo shoots. The tips of various species of bamboo, these ivory-colored rectangular shoots are flat and crisp. Fresh shoots should be washed, peeled, and then sliced or shredded according to the recipe. Canned shoots come whole, sliced, or shredded, and should be thoroughly rinsed with cold fresh water before using.

Black mushrooms, Chinese. *See* Shiitake mushrooms.

Bok choy. With long, smooth, milky-white stems that are topped with crinkly green leaves, bok choy looks similar to celery. Crisp, sweet, and juicy, it is generally shredded and added to stir-fry dishes.

Chili peppers. Little chili peppers contribute color, flavor, and varying degrees of heat to dishes. Chili peppers range from mild to very hot, sweet to acidic, and fresh to dry. Although there are over a hundred varieties of chili peppers, only a few are readily available in most grocery stores. The most common varieties are the large, mild Anaheims and the hot to very hot jalapeños. Sometimes, I am able to get fresh Vietnamese and Thai peppers at the farmer's market near my home. These tiny peppers are rated as being ten times hotter than jalapeños!

Chinese cabbage. *See* Napa cabbage.

Chinese mushrooms. *See* Shiitake mushrooms.

Ginger root. One of the most popular seasonings used in Chinese cooking, fresh ginger root is found in the produce section of most grocery stores. Fresh roots have smooth tan skins and can be used immediately or preserved for later use. Wash only that part of the root you are about to use, peel away the outer skin from that portion (actually, I prefer to leave the skin on, which I find saves time and adds more flavor), and cut or grate the flavorful root. Be sure to wrap the remaining ginger root in plastic wrap and store in the refrigerator where it will keep for several weeks. (Ginger that has been kept out too long will develop a bluish tinge where it was cut.)

Green onions. Also called scallions, green onions are immature onions that have not developed an outer skin. Green onions are sold with their long green leaves attached and can be up to ten inches long. They are sweet and mild-tasting, and are delicious both raw and cooked. Sometimes I replant the base of these vegetables, so I always have fresh ones on hand!

Kelp. Also called seaweed, kelp is a nutritious sea vegetable that is a good source of iron. Kelp comes in threads, sheets, strips, and granules.

Most varieties are dry and must be soaked in warm water and softened before using. Other varieties have been roasted and seasoned, and require no presoaking. This type can be added directly to dishes.

Kelp granules often come packaged in shaker containers. Maine Coast Sea Vegetables makes a kelp granule shake that contains only 42 milligrams of sodium per half-teaspoon serving. Dry kelp can be stored in a pantry.

Jalapeño peppers. *See* Chili peppers.

Leeks. These large onion-like vegetables are often more than twelve inches long with flat green leaves that taper only slightly to a white bulb. Both the leaves and bulbs are used to complement seafood, tofu, and meat dishes. Fresh leeks, which are filled with grit and sand, must be thoroughly cleaned before they are used.

Mushrooms. *See* Shiitake mushrooms.

Napa cabbage. Also called Chinese cabbage, Napa has crinkled pale-green leaves that are tightly packed. Often shredded and used in a variety of dishes, this cabbage requires little cooking.

Scallions. *See* Green onions.

Seaweed. *See* Kelp.

Shiitake mushrooms. Also called Chinese black mushrooms, shiitake are sold in many American grocery stores. These mushrooms have a savory, meaty flavor and are reputed to possess medicinal qualities—many believe these mushrooms prevent cancer! Although fresh shiitake are available, the dried variety is most common. Before using the dried mushrooms, they must be hydrated (*see* Hydrating Dried Mushrooms on page 37). For the recipes in this book, you can substitute domestic fresh white mushrooms for the shiitake.

Water chestnuts. The crunchiest of vegetables, this pale, almost translucent tuber, is most often found canned. Before using, discard the water from the can and rinse the chestnuts in fresh water. They add crunchy crispness to stir-fry dishes, salads, and soups. Fat-free water chestnuts are very low in sodium.

GRAINS, NOODLES, AND SOY PRODUCTS

Just because a food is fat-free does not mean it is good for you. Fat-free products made from refined white flour and refined grains provide few nutrients and can actually deplete some of your body's nutrients if eaten in excess. Whole grains and whole grain products, on the other hand, contain a great many nutrients including vitamin E, zinc, magnesium, chromium, and potassium. Whole grain products also add fiber to our diets. Fat from fiber provides a feeling of fullness, making our meals more satisfying. Fiber also helps maintain blood sugar levels, which keeps us from feeling hungry.

Many of the following products, which are used in this book, are readily available in grocery stores, while others can be found in health food stores and Asian markets.

Bean curd. *See* Tofu.

Bean paste. *See* Miso.

Glutinous rice. Also called sweet rice, short-grained glutinous rice cooks up softer and stickier than other varieties. It is used in all types of dishes.

Miso. A fermented soyfood, this thick paste made from soybeans and/or grains is called miso in Japan and bean paste in China. Although there are a number of miso varieties, the dark-colored red or brown miso is the type primarily used in Chinese cooking. Strong, salty flavored miso can replace salt in many recipes, especially soups. Two tablespoons of low-sodium miso are equivalent to about a half teaspoon of salt.

A good source of amino acids and some vitamins and minerals, miso is also low in fat and calories. Recent scientific studies indicate that daily use of miso may lower cholesterol, alkalize the blood, and cancel the effects of some carcinogens. It is also believed that miso is able to counteract the effects of radiation exposure and neutralize the effects of smoking and environmental pollution. Unpasteurized miso is abundant in helpful lactic-acid bacteria and enzymes that aid in digestion.

Look for miso brands that are low in sodium and preservative-free. Some varieties are almost one-third salt. Organic Gourmet, Eden, and Cold Mountain brands are good choices.

Noodles. *See* Rice noodles; Whole wheat noodles.

Rice. *See* Glutinous Rice.

Spring roll wrappers. Made from rice flour and water, these delicate wrappers are beautifully translucent and excellent for making spring rolls. To soften spring roll wrappers, they must be soaked for two to three minutes in warm water. Tightly wrapped, the dry wrappers can be stored up to three months or longer in the pantry.

Rice noodles. Made from rice flour, these thin, flat translucent noodles, are very similar to linguini and can be purchased in both fresh and dry forms. The dried variety must be softened in warm water for five to seven minutes before cooking. Rice noodles are popularly used in soups or cold noodle dishes. Fresh rice noodles are very popular in southeast Asian cooking.

Sweet rice. *See* Glutinous rice.

Tofu. Cholesterol-free, tofu or bean curd is a versatile soy product that is high in protein and calcium. In addition, tofu contains all eight essential amino acids. Having very little taste, tofu absorbs the flavors of its surrounding ingredients. Fresh or baked, tofu can be silken, firm, or extra-firm in texture.

Recently, fresh tofu with a very low fat content has appeared on store shelves. I prefer to use White Wave and Mori-Nu brands. Mori-Nu's firm and extra-firm tofu has only 1 gram of fat per 3-ounce serving.

Whole wheat noodles. Noodles made from whole wheat flour come fresh or dry. The fresh noodles should be stored in the refrigerator or frozen for long-term storage. Whole wheat noodles are used in stir-fry dishes and soups. Any fresh or dry whole wheat spaghetti or fettuccine noodle is a good substitute.

SAUCES, SPICES, HERBS, AND FLAVORINGS

Flavorful herbs and spices, as well as a variety of sauces can enhance a dish without contributing significant amounts of fat or sodium. Most of the following ingredients, which are called for in this book, are readily found in most grocery stores, health food stores, and Asian markets.

Agar-agar. A vegetable gelatin made from several varieties of red seaweed, agar-agar contains no fat and zero calories! Commonly used with vegetables and stocks to make molded aspics, agar is also used in puddings, pie fillings, and gelatin desserts. It is a common substitute for the pectin in jams and jellies. Even without refrigeration, agar sets quickly as it cools and seals in the natural flavor of the fruits or vegetables used in the dish.

Top Right: Pan-Fried Cheese-and-Spinach Dumplings (page 50)
Left: Broiled Curried Chicken Spring Rolls (page 38)
Bottom Right: Steamed Shrimp Dumplings (page 47)
Hot Dipping Sauce and Mustard Dipping Sauce (page 56)

Top Left: **Curried Rice with Green Peas (page 61)**
Top Right: **Simple Egg Drop Soup (page 22)**
Bottom: **Kung Po Beef (page 111)**

Homemade Chili Paste

Chili paste adds a spark of heat to any dish. Available in most Asian markets, this spicy seasoning is easy to make yourself. As an added bonus, it has no fat, cholesterol, or calories.

1. Coat a nonstick frying pan with cooking spray. Add the chili and garlic, and sauté until the garlic begins to brown.

2. Dissolve the cornstarch in the soy sauce and add it to the pan along with the wine. Stir the ingredients together.

3. Transfer the cooled mixture to an airtight container and store in the refrigerator.

4. Stir the chili paste before using it.

1 1/2 tablespoons minced fresh or dried chili peppers

1 tablespoon minced garlic

1 1/2 teaspoons cornstarch

2 tablespoons low-sodium soy sauce

2 tablespoons cooking wine

Broth. Chicken, beef, and vegetable broths are available in low-sodium, fat-free varieties. Healthy Choice brand and Shelton's are good choices.

Chili paste. Fresh ground chili paste contains red or green chilies and a combination of onions, garlic, and other seasonings. Commonly sold in jars, chili paste adds a spark of heat to any dish. Many commercial varieties are high in sodium, so be sure to check labels. I prefer the flavorful yet low-sodium chili paste made by Huy Fong Foods. (For Homemade Chili Paste *see* recipe above.)

Chili pepper flakes. These dried and flaked red chilies can be very hot. Dehydration seems to intensify their flavor. Properly sealed in an airtight container, these hot flakes can be used for a long time. Be sure to keep them out of your children's reach.

Chinese parsley. *See* Cilantro.

Chinese vinegar. *See* Rice vinegar.

Cilantro. Also called Chinese parsley, cilantro has a uniquely fragrant, slightly musky flavor. Like parsley, fresh cilantro is quite perishable. It is a flavorful addition to a variety of Chinese-style foods.

Cornstarch. Cornstarch is frequently used as a thickener for sauces in Chinese dishes. Always mix cornstarch with a little liquid before adding it to the other ingredients.

Curry powder. Curry powder is really a combination of many spices including turmeric, cumin, and cardamom. Commercially made curry powder does not compare to the full-flavored imported brands from India. Once opened, curry powder should be used within three to four months for maximum flavor.

Five-spice powder. This ground spice is a common ingredient in many Oriental dishes. It is a variety of spices in various combinations with anise and cinnamon being the constant ingredients. In addition, five-spice powder most commonly includes fennel seeds, cloves, ginger root, licorice, nutmeg, and Szechuan peppercorns. Five-spice powder is fat- and sodium-free.

Garlic. My husband says that the only thing worse than too much garlic is not enough garlic! Used properly, garlic imparts a wonderful aroma and taste and acts to support other more prominent ingredients in a dish.

Once garlic was available in fresh and powdered forms only. Today, jars of chopped or minced garlic that has been preserved in oil are also available. Fresh garlic, of course, is the best choice. Choose plump, firm bulbs with papery skin that is firmly attached. Do not refrigerate fresh garlic, rather store it in a cool, dry place with good ventilation. Once fresh garlic begins to sprout, discard it, as this signifies that much of its flavor and pungency are gone.

Herb seasoning blend. This salt-free combination of flavorful herbs and spices is commonly used as a salt substitute. Mrs. Dash and Spike are two well-known brands.

Honey mustard. Made with water, rice flour, vinegar, honey, corn syrup, soy sauce, and ground mustard seeds, honey mustard has a pungent sweetness that is ideal in stir-fry dishes, sauces, and marinades. It also makes a wonderful barbecue glaze. The Rice Road brand, which has only 270 milligrams of sodium per tablespoon, contains no preservatives or MSG.

Mrs. Dash seasoning. *See* Herb seasoning blend.

Mustard sauce. Used in dipping sauces and marinades, mustard sauce is made primarily of ground mustard seeds, vinegar, water, sugar, garlic, and other spices. Mustard sauce comes in sweet, hot, and extra-hot varieties. I use Dynasty brand, which is fat-free and contains only 35 milligrams of sodium per teaspoon. Refrigerate after opening.

Peanut butter. Peanut butter is often used as a sauce ingredient in southeast Asian dishes. Unfortunately, peanut butter is full of fat and calories. But this does not mean you should eliminate it from your diet. Remember, you can and should eat some fat in order to get essential fatty acids. Peanut butter, like other nut and seed products, supplies some of these essential fats. Most leading brands, however, contain small amounts of both partially and fully hydrogenated vegetable oils to prevent the oil from separating and rising to the top. Top brands also contain added sugar and salt. Many reduced-fat brands of peanut butter substitute corn syrup or similar products for part of the fat. The result is a peanut butter with about 25-percent less fat, but little or no difference in calories.

The most natural peanut butter is made from roasted peanuts with no added hydrogenated fats. Two delicious choices are Smucker's Natural, which contains no added fats, and Arrowhead Mills Easy Spreading, which contains a small amount of lecithin. Lecithin, a nutritious by-product of soybean oil refining, prevents the peanut butter from separating, giving it a smooth consistency.

Pepper. Both black and white pepper varieties come ground or in whole peppercorns, which must be ground in a peppermill. I prefer the whole pepper when a coarse grind is desired.

Rice Dream beverage. Made from organic brown rice, safflower oil, and sea salt, this nondairy, mild-flavored beverage has a consistency similar to skim milk. It may be used in some recipes to replace soymilk or dairy milk.

Rice vinegar. Made from fermented rice, rice vinegar (also called Chinese vinegar) is stronger flavored than most domestic varieties. It is commonly found in the ethnic-food section of most grocery stores. Domestic white vinegar can be used as a substitute.

Rice wine. As its name implies, rice wine is made from rice. It is an often-used ingredient in Chinese-style cooking. The higher-quality varieties are generally used as a beverage. You can easily substitute rice wine with sake, Scotch whiskey, dry sherry, or white vermouth. I find adding rice wine to seafood dishes prevents the dishes from taking on a "fishy" flavor.

Salt. *See* What About Salt? on page 17.

Sesame shakes. Eden brand sesame shakes come in jars with shaker tops for easy sprinkling on foods. Each sesame shake contains roasted, chopped organic sesame seeds that are combined with other flavorful ingredients. Different varieties contain sea salt, seaweed, and garlic. Each shake has only 40 milligrams of sodium per teaspoon.

Soy sauce. Generally speaking, soy sauce is fat-free but quite high in sodium. The good news is you can find this flavorful sauce in low-sodium varieties. I recommend the China Dragon brand extra-lite soy sauce, which contains only 200 milligrams of sodium per tablespoon. Kikkoman Lite and La Choy Lite are other good reduced-sodium choices.

Sweet-and-sour sauce. Most varieties of sweet-and-sour sauce are made from pineapples, tomatoes, sugar, and rice vinegar, and usually contain only 1 gram of fat and about 140 milligrams of sodium per 2 tablespoons. It adds zesty sweetness to dips and marinades.

Vinegar. *See* Rice vinegar.

OILS AND COOKING SPRAYS

Even in a low-fat kitchen, a little bit of oil is sometimes necessary to enhance flavor, prevent sticking, or promote browning. The following products will be invaluable in many of your low-fat Chinese cooking adventures.

Canola oil. Low in saturated fats and rich in monounsaturated fats, canola oil also contains a good amount of linolenic acid, an essential omega-3 type fat. (For more information on omega-3 oils, *see* discussion under Fish and Seafood, beginning on page 8). Canola oil's mild, bland taste makes it a good all-purpose oil for cooking and baking when you want no interfering flavors. Like all oils, canola oil should be used sparingly to limit calories.

Chili oil. Also called hot oil, this combination of chili flakes, canola oil, garlic, soy sauce, and rice vinegar can really spice up a dish. The flavor of chili oil is so intense that a very small amount can give a dish significant flavor without adding much fat. Found in most Asian markets and some grocery stores, chili oil is also easy to make yourself. (*See* recipe for Homemade Chili Oil on page 16).

Cooking spray. Nonstick vegetable-oil cooking sprays, which are available in unflavored and in butter and olive oil flavors, are pure fat. But because the amount produced in a one-second spray is quite small, these products add an insignificant amount of fat to a recipe. For the low-fat cook, nonstick cooking sprays are very useful to encourage the browning of foods and to prevent foods from sticking to pots and pans. I recommend PAM Olive Oil No Stick, Mazola No Stick, and Wesson No

Warning About Cooking Sprays

Cooking sprays are easy to use, but it is important to remember that the spray is flammable. ***Always apply the spray to a cool pan.*** *Allow the cooking spray to heat up a few seconds before adding the food. This basic step will result in food that is crisp, tender, and tasty.*

Stick cooking sprays. When a recipe directs you to both grease and flour a pan, use Baker's Joy spray, which combines oil and flour in one product.

Olive oil. Considered a "healthful" oil because it is low in saturated fat and does not promote heart disease, olive oil is used sparingly in a few Chinese dishes. However, like all oils, olive oil is pure fat, and contains 120 calories per tablespoon. Some of the recipes in this book do include small amounts of olive oil—just enough to enhance flavor.

Always be sure to use extra-virgin olive oil, which is the least processed and most flavorful kind available. Do not choose "light" olive oil.

In this case, light refers to flavor, which is mild and bland compared with that of extra-virgin oils. This means you would have to use more oil to obtain the same amount of flavor—not a good bargain.

Sesame oil. Strong, nutty-flavored sesame oil is a popular ingredient in a large number of Oriental-style dishes. Like olive oil, sesame oil is so flavorful that just a little bit goes a long way. Used in small amounts, this ingredient will add a distinctive taste to dishes without adding a significant amount of fat. As high heat causes sesame oil's flavor to evaporate, always add it to a dish at the end of its cooking time.

Homemade Chili Oil

If you love really spicy Chinese food, hot chili oil should be one of your kitchen staples. As this oil may be hard to find in many grocery stores, why not make your own to always have on hand? Depending on your tolerance for hot spices, you can choose varying amounts of fresh or dried, and mild to very hot chili peppers. I recommend fresh jalapeño chilies, which are widely available and fall in the middle of the "hot list" for chili peppers. Hot chili oil can be used to flavor ingredients as they cook, or as a condiment to add to a dish before it is served. Although its fat content cannot be denied, only a drop or two is necessary for flavoring most dishes.

¼ cup minced fresh or dried chili peppers

8 cloves garlic, crushed

3 tablespoons canola or corn oil

¼ cup low-sodium soy sauce

2 tablespoons rice vinegar

1. Place the peppers and garlic in a heat-resistant bowl and set aside.

2. Heat the oil in a small pan over medium heat until quite hot. (Do not let the oil smoke.) Carefully pour the hot oil over the garlic and peppers. (As the peppers may release a strong burning vapor that can be painful to inhale, it may be wise to do this near an open window or exhaust fan.)

3. Allow the mixture to cool before adding the remaining ingredients.

4. Place the flavored oil in a glass jar, seal tightly, and store in the refrigerator where it will keep indefinitely.

EGG WHITES AND EGG SUBSTITUTES

Anyone who cooks knows the value of eggs. Eggs are used extensively in Chinese cooking, but they are loaded with cholesterol and contain some fat as well. For this reason, most of the recipes in this book that require eggs call for egg whites or fat-free egg substitute. Just how great are your savings in cholesterol and fat? One large egg contains 80 calories, 5 grams of fat, and 210 milligrams of cholesterol. The equivalent amount of fat-free egg substitute contains 20 to 30 calories, no fat, and no cholesterol. Because they have been pasteurized (heat treated), egg substitutes are safe to use uncooked in dips and dressings.

When selecting an egg substitute, look for a fat-free brand like Egg Beaters, Scramblers, Better'n Eggs, or Nu Laid. If you choose another brand, be sure to check the label carefully, as some egg substitutes contain vegetable oil. One large egg is equivalent to 3 tablespoons of egg substitute.

WHAT ABOUT SALT?

A combination of sodium and chloride, salt enhances the flavors of many foods. However, most health experts recommend a maximum of 2,400 milligrams of sodium (about one teaspoon of salt) per day. No salt is added to the recipes in this book. A minimal use of salt-laden processed ingredients, such as soy sauce, as well as a wise use of herbs and spices, keeps the salt content under control without compromising taste.

By limiting the salt, you will enjoy more of the food's freshness and flavor. Use your creativity (and sense of adventure) to bring a dish flavor. For instance, use fresh lemon juice, especially in fish and seafood dishes. Enhance the appeal of some foods with mustard sauce, sesame seeds or shakes, five-spice powder, chili paste, cilantro, or basil.

NATURAL INGREDIENTS AND FAT

Even though a recipe may not contain an obviously fatty ingredient, such as butter, oil, margarine, nuts, or chocolate, it may still contain a small amount of fat (less than 1 gram). This is because many natural ingredients contain some fat. Whole grains, for example, store a small amount of oil in their germ, the center portion of the grain. This oil is very beneficial because it is loaded with vitamin E, an antioxidant. The germ also provides an abundance of vitamins and minerals. Products made from refined grains and refined flours—ingredients that have been stripped of the germ—do have slightly less fat than whole grain versions, but they also have far less nutrients.

Other ingredients, too, naturally contain small amounts of fat. For instance, fruits and vegetables, like grains, contain some oil. And, again, the oil provides many important nutrients. Olives, nuts, and lean meats also contribute fat to some recipes. However, when used in small quantities, the amount of fat is insignificant.

CONCLUSION

Now that you understand the importance of controlling dietary fat and are familiar with the best ingredients to use in low-fat and fat-free Chinese dishes, it's time to put this knowledge to use. Soon you will discover how to use these ingredients to create great-tasting, sure-to-please family favorites.

Remember, cooking is an art. Much as the conductor of an orchestra brings together a combination of different sounds and rhythms, the cook brings together a combination of foods and cooking techniques to create a symphony for the palate.

2. Heartwarming Soups

In China, soup is not served as an appetizer. Rather, it is placed in a large bowl that is set in the middle of the table. The Chinese, who are not in the habit of drinking any beverage with their meals, help themselves to the soup at any time. Traditionally, tea is then served at the meal's end.

Although sweet soups are served as popular desserts in some parts of China, basically, Chinese soups fall into two main categories: light and thick. Light soups are usually clear with a chicken, pork, or vegetable broth base. Popular varieties include egg drop, wonton, and seafood soups. Thick, savory soups, which are thickened with cornstarch (not milk or cream) are often served as a main course.

These include hot-and-sour soups and soups made with tofu (bean curd).

This chapter presents soups that are low in fat and easy to make. Most of the ingredients can be prepared in advance and cooked just before serving.

Many traditional Chinese soups call for chicken or pork broth, which is made by cooking the bones and fatty parts of the animal in water for several hours. This time-consuming process results in broth that is high in fat and cholesterol. Instead, the following recipes combine fresh ingredients, flavorful spices, and low-sodium fat-free broths. This combination results in nutritious soups that are satisfying and delicious.

Curried Beef Noodle Soup

1. Bring the water, broth, and curry powder to a boil in a large pot.

2. Add the noodles and bring to a second boil. Reduce the heat to low and cook for 2 minutes. Add the miso (if using fresh miso, dilute it in a little water before adding it to the pot). Continue to simmer for 2 minutes.

3. Add the sesame oil. Garnish with cilantro and serve.

Yield: *6 servings*

3 cups cold water

2 cups low-sodium fat-free beef broth

1 tablespoon curry powder

3 cups cooked rice noodles

1 tablespoon fresh or instant low-sodium miso

1 teaspoon sesame oil

3 sprigs fresh cilantro, chopped

NUTRITIONAL FACTS (PER 1-CUP SERVING)

Calories: 172 Carbohydrates: 34.1 g Cholesterol: 0 mg
Fat: 1.9 g Fiber: 0.2 g Protein: 5.3 g Sodium: 179 mg

Tofu Hot-and-Sour Soup

1. Bring the water to a boil in a large pot. Add the mushrooms, tofu, and bamboo shoots. Boil for 2 minutes.

2. Reduce the heat to low and add the vinegar, soy sauce, and chili flakes. Dissolve the cornstarch in a little water and add it to the pot. Simmer 3 to 4 minutes while stirring occasionally. Stir in the sesame oil.

3. Garnish with green onion and black pepper before serving.

Yield: *8 servings*

6 cups cold water

8 shiitake mushroom caps, sliced (if using dried variety, *see* hydrating instructions on page 37)

8 ounces firm low-fat tofu, cut into 1/2-inch cubes

1/4 cup bamboo shoots

1 1/2 tablespoons rice vinegar

3 tablespoons low-sodium soy sauce

1/4 teaspoon chili pepper flakes

2 tablespoons cornstarch

1 teaspoon sesame oil

1 green onion, minced

1/4 teaspoon ground black pepper

NUTRITIONAL FACTS (PER 1-CUP SERVING)

Calories: 39 Carbohydrates: 5.4 g Cholesterol: 0 mg
Fat: 0.9 g Fiber: 0.3 g Protein: 2.6 g Sodium: 103 mg

Tofu and Spinach Soup

Yield: 6 servings

5 cups cold water

8 ounces firm low-fat tofu, cut into ½-inch cubes

1 tablespoon fresh or instant low-sodium miso

8 ounces fresh spinach, washed and coarsely chopped

6 springs fresh cilantro, minced

1. In a large pot, bring the water to a boil. Add the tofu and miso (if using fresh miso, dilute it in a little water before adding it to the pot). Bring to a second boil and cook 3 minutes.

2. Add the spinach and cilantro. When the soup reaches a boil again, remove it from the stove and serve immediately.

NUTRITIONAL FACTS (PER 1-CUP SERVING)
Calories: 29 Carbohydrates: 1.8 g Cholesterol: 0 mg
Fat: 0.6 g Fiber: 1 g Protein: 4.3 g Sodium: 190 mg

Simple Egg Drop Soup

Yield: 6 servings

6 cups cold water

2 tablespoons cornstarch

1 tablespoon fresh or instant low-sodium miso

8 ounces firm low-fat tofu, cut into ½-inch cubes

1 egg, well beaten

1 teaspoon sesame oil

2 green onions, minced

2 sprigs fresh cilantro, minced

I have found that a whole beaten egg forms much better threads than egg substitute in this soup. The choice, however, is yours.

1. In a large pot, bring the water to a boil. Dissolve the cornstarch in a little water, then add it to the pot along with the miso. (If using fresh miso, dilute it in a little water before adding it to the pot.)

2. Add the tofu and bring to a second boil.

3. Slowly pour in the beaten egg, while stirring the soup in one direction with a chopstick or fork so the egg cooks into threads. Remove from the heat.

4. Stir in the sesame oil. Garnish with green onions and cilantro and serve.

NUTRITIONAL FACTS (PER 1-CUP SERVING)
Calories: 52 Carbohydrates: 3.6 g Cholesterol: 36 mg
Fat: 2 g Fiber: 0 g Protein: 4.3 g Sodium: 173 mg

Meatball and Spinach Soup

You can substitute lean ground beef or pork for the turkey in this soup.

1. Bring the water and miso to a boil in a large pot. (If using fresh miso, dilute it in a little water before adding it to the pot).

2. While waiting for the water to boil, prepare the meatballs. In a large bowl, thoroughly mix together all of the meatball ingredients. Form the mixture into teaspoon-sized meatballs (about 12).

3. When the water comes to a boil, add the meatballs, one at a time. Reduce the heat, and simmer for 8 minutes.

4. Add the spinach and bring to a boil. Cook for 4 minutes. Serve hot.

NUTRITIONAL FACTS (PER 1-CUP SERVING WITH 2 MEATBALLS)

Calories: 60 Carbohydrates: 6.1 g Cholesterol: 7 mg
Fat: 0.6 g Fiber: 3.4 g Protein: 7.9 g Sodium: 238 mg

Yield: *6 servings*

5 cups cold water

1 tablespoon fresh or instant low-sodium miso

1½ pounds fresh spinach, washed and coarsely chopped

MEATBALLS

4 ounces lean ground turkey

1 tablespoon minced fresh ginger

1 tablespoon minced fresh garlic

2 green onions, minced

2 teaspoons cornstarch

1 egg white

½ teaspoon Eden Foods sesame shake, or chopped sesame seeds

⅛ teaspoon chili pepper flakes

Colorful Spicy Vegetable Soup

Yield: 6 servings

3 cups cold water

2 cups low-sodium fat-free vegetable broth

1 teaspoon commercial chili paste or Homemade Chili Paste (page 13)

5 cloves garlic, minced

1 small green bell pepper, cut into thin strips

1 small red bell pepper, cut into thin strips

1/4 cup thinly sliced Napa cabbage

1 teaspoon sesame oil

1. Combine the water and broth in a large pot. Add the chili paste and stir to dissolve. Add the garlic and bring to a boil. Cook for 2 minutes.

2. Add the bell peppers and cabbage. Bring to a second boil and cook for 5 minutes.

3. Add the sesame oil and serve.

NUTRITIONAL FACTS (PER 1-CUP SERVING)

Calories: 32 Carbohydrates: 6 g Cholesterol: 0 mg
Fat: 0.8 g Fiber: 0.9 g Protein: 0.8 g Sodium: 36 mg

Curried Vegetable and Tofu Soup

Yield: 6 servings

3 cups cold water

2 cups low-sodium fat-free vegetable broth

1 tablespoon curry powder

8 ounces firm low-fat tofu, cut into 1/2-inch cubes

1 cup green peas

1/2 cup chopped celery

1 tablespoon fresh or instant low-sodium miso

1/2 teaspoon sesame oil

2 green onions, minced

1. Bring the water, broth, and curry powder to a boil in a large pot.

2. Add the tofu, peas, and celery, and bring to a second boil. Reduce the heat to low and cook for 5 minutes. Add the miso (if using fresh miso, dilute it in a little water before adding it to the pot). Continue to simmer for 2 minutes.

3. Add the sesame oil. Garnish with green onions and serve.

NUTRITIONAL FACTS (PER 1-CUP SERVING)

Calories: 63 Carbohydrates: 8.4 g Cholesterol: 0 mg
Fat: 1 g Fiber: 1.7 g Protein: 5 g Sodium: 180 mg

Spicy Shrimp and Corn Soup

1. Place the water, wine, ginger, and chili pepper flakes in a large pot. Dissolve the cornstarch in a little water and add it to the pot. Bring to a boil for 2 minutes then reduce the heat.

2. Add the corn, shrimp, and soy sauce. Cook for 3 minutes.

3. Add the sesame shake and black pepper and cook for 2 more minutes.

4. Stir in the sesame oil and serve.

NUTRITIONAL FACTS (PER 1-CUP SERVING)
Calories: 139 Carbohydrates: 21.3 g Cholesterol: 57 mg
Fat: 1.2 g Fiber: 1.8 g Protein: 10.7 g Sodium: 138 mg

Yield: 6 servings

6 cups cold water

1$\frac{1}{2}$ teaspoons cooking wine

1 tablespoon minced fresh ginger

$\frac{1}{4}$ teaspoon chili pepper flakes

1 tablespoon cornstarch

3 cups fresh or frozen corn kernels

8 ounces small shrimp, cooked

2 tablespoons low-sodium soy sauce

$\frac{3}{4}$ teaspoon Eden Foods sesame shake, or chopped sesame seeds

$\frac{3}{4}$ teaspoon ground black pepper

$\frac{1}{2}$ teaspoon sesame oil

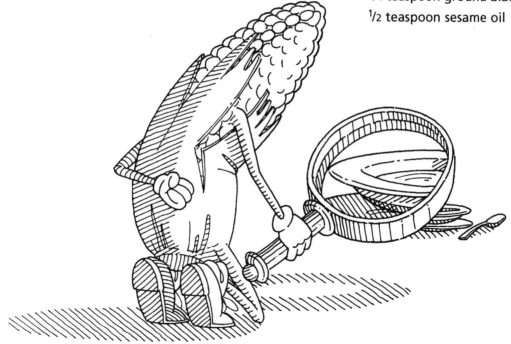

Fish Onion Soup

1. Combine the marinade ingredients in a bowl. Add the fish and toss well to coat. Cover and refrigerate 20 minutes.

2. In a large saucepan, bring the water and broth to a boil. Add the onion and cook for 2 minutes.

3. Add the marinated fish, bring to a second boil, and cook for 4 minutes.

4. Add the sesame oil. Garnish with green onion and cilantro and serve.

NUTRITIONAL FACTS (PER 1-CUP SERVING)
Calories: 54 Carbohydrates: 6 g Cholesterol: 9 mg
Fat: 1 g Fiber: 0.8 g Protein: 4.4 g Sodium: 95 mg

Yield: 6 servings

6 ounces sole, flounder, or other white fish, cut into 1½-inch cubes

3 cups water

2 cups low-sodium fat-free vegetable broth

1 large white onion, coarsely chopped

1 teaspoon sesame oil

1 green onion, chopped

2 sprigs fresh cilantro, chopped

MARINADE

4 teaspoons rice wine

2 tablespoons low-sodium soy sauce

½ teaspoon minced fresh ginger

½ teaspoon five-spice powder

Tomato Egg-Flower Soup

I have found that a whole beaten egg forms much better threads than egg substitute in this soup. The choice, however, is yours.

1. Combine the water and broth in a large pot. Dissolve the cornstarch in a little water and add it to the pot. Bring to a boil.

2. Add the tomatoes and bring to a second boil.

3. Slowly pour in the beaten egg, while stirring the soup in one direction with a chopstick or fork so the egg cooks into threads. Remove from the heat.

4. Add the sesame shake and sesame oil. Garnish with cilantro and serve.

Yield: *6 servings*

3 cups water

2 cups low-sodium fat-free chicken broth

1 teaspoon cornstarch

2 large tomatoes, diced

1 egg, well beaten

2 teaspoons Eden Foods sesame shake, or chopped sesame seeds

1 teaspoon sesame oil

2 sprigs fresh cilantro, minced

NUTRITIONAL FACTS (PER 1-CUP SERVING)

Calories: 45 Carbohydrates: 2.5 g Cholesterol: 36 mg
Fat: 1.8 g Fiber: 0.6 g Protein: 2 g Sodium: 46 mg

Chicken and Potato Soup

1. Bring the broth, wine, potatoes, ginger, garlic, sesame shake, and pepper to boil in a large pot.

2. Reduce the heat to medium and simmer, partially covered, until the potatoes are tender (about 30 minutes).

3. Bring to a second boil. Add the chicken and cook for 3 minutes.

4. Garnish with cilantro and serve.

Yield: *6 servings*

5 cups low-sodium fat-free chicken broth

1 1/2 teaspoons rice wine

2 medium-sized potatoes, peeled and cut into 1 1/2-inch chunks

6 thin ginger slices

4 cloves garlic, crushed

2 teaspoons Eden Foods sesame shake, or chopped sesame seeds

1/4 teaspoon ground black pepper

1/4 cup cooked chicken strips (*see page 9*)

3 sprigs fresh cilantro, minced

NUTRITIONAL FACTS (PER 1-CUP SERVING)

Calories: 77 Carbohydrates: 7.5 g Cholesterol: 4 mg
Fat: 0.6 g Fiber: 1 g Protein: 4 g Sodium: 79 mg

Chicken Rice Soup

Yield: 8 servings

12 ounces skinless chicken
   breasts, cut into paper-thin
   slices

6 cups low-sodium fat-free
   chicken broth

2 tablespoons cornstarch

1/3 cup uncooked rice, washed
   and drained

3/4 cup thinly sliced carrots

3/4 cup finely chopped celery

1/4 teaspoon chili pepper flakes

MARINADE

2 tablespoons rice wine

2 tablespoons low-sodium soy
   sauce

1 teaspoon minced fresh ginger

3/4 teaspoon sesame oil

Chilling the chicken in the freezer about 30 minutes makes it easier to slice.

1. Combine the marinade ingredients in a bowl. Add the chicken and toss well to coat. Cover the bowl and refrigerate 30 minutes.

2. Place the broth in a large pot. Dissolve the cornstarch in a little water, then add it to the pot along with the rice and carrots. Bring to a boil.

3. Reduce the heat to medium-low and simmer the ingredients for 15 minutes, while stirring occasionally.

4. Add the marinated chicken, celery, and chili pepper flakes. Cook another 5 minutes or until the rice is tender. Serve hot or cold.

NUTRITIONAL FACTS (PER 1-CUP SERVING)

Calories: 100 Carbohydrates: 10.1 g Cholesterol: 13 mg
Fat: 0.8 g Fiber: 0.8 g Protein: 7.8 g Sodium: 130 mg

A Time-Saving Tip

Most recipes call for ingredients that need to be prepared in some way—garlic may need to be minced, peppers diced, or tomatoes cubed. Whenever possible, have such ingredients ready before you begin cooking. This will allow you to go through the cooking process quickly and easily.

Some vegetables and herbs can be prepared days in advance. Items such as fresh ginger, garlic, and scallions can all be diced, minced, or crushed, then stored in separate airtight containers and placed in the refrigerator where they will keep for several days. For maximum freshness, thoroughly dry the ingredients before cutting them.

Green Tea and Beef Soup

Check your local health food store or the foreign-food section of your grocery store for the dry-roasted seaweed (kelp) and the miso called for in this recipe.

1. In a large pot, bring the water to a boil. Place the tea in a tea ball and add it to the pot. Reduce the heat to low, cover, and simmer 10 minutes.

2. Add the seaweed, beef, and bean sprouts. Bring to boil while occasionally stirring. Add the miso (if using fresh miso, dilute it in a little water before adding it to the pot), reduce the heat to low, and simmer about 5 minutes.

3. Remove the tea ball and discard the tea leaves.

4. Garnish with green onion and serve.

Yield: 6 servings

5 cups cold water

2 teaspoons green tea

6 pieces (2-x-3$\frac{1}{2}$-inch) dry-roasted seaweed

$\frac{1}{4}$ cup cooked beef strips (*see page 9*)

1 cup bean sprouts

1 tablespoon fresh or instant low-sodium miso

2 green onions, minced

NUTRITIONAL FACTS (PER 1-CUP SERVING)
Calories: 46 Carbohydrates: 6.3 g Cholesterol: 8 mg
Fat: 0.3 g Fiber: 1.5 g Protein: 4.8 g Sodium: 413 mg

Crabmeat and Corn Soup

1. In a large pot, bring the water to a boil. Add the crabmeat, corn, and ginger. Boil for 2 minutes.

2. Reduce the heat and add the sesame oil, black pepper, and five-spice powder. Simmer 2 minutes.

3. Garnish with green onion and serve.

Yield: 6 servings

5 cups cold water

8 ounces crabmeat, flaked*

4 cups fresh or frozen corn kernels

1$\frac{1}{2}$ teaspoons minced fresh ginger

1 teaspoon sesame oil

$\frac{1}{2}$ teaspoon ground black pepper

$\frac{1}{4}$ teaspoon five-spice powder

2 green onions, minced

* Can use artificial variety.

NUTRITIONAL FACTS (PER 1-CUP SERVING)
Calories: 156 Carbohydrates: 26.1 g Cholesterol: 22 mg
Fat: 2.4 g Fiber: 2.9 g Protein: 7.9 g Sodium: 91 mg

3. Sensational Spring Rolls and Dumplings

Wonderful party fare, spring rolls and dumplings are great to serve as appetizers and side dishes. They are a perfect addition to any buffet table. Unfortunately, these delicious items have always had a reputation for being high in fat. But with a few ingredient adjustments along with sensible cooking methods, I will show you how to make fat-free or very low-fat versions of these delightful treats.

Spring Rolls

In China, spring rolls—often called egg rolls—are traditionally eaten in celebration of the Chinese New Year. The name "spring roll" comes from its association with the new year and the approaching season of spring.

Spring rolls have always been quite popular among my American friends. However, the high-fat content of the deep-fried varieties served in most Americanized Chinese restaurants have caused many people to stop eating them. Well, good news is here. There is no need to deprive yourself of these delicious rolls any longer. On the following pages, I present recipes for low-fat spring rolls with delightfully flavorful and nutritious fillings, complete with easy-to-follow preparation and cooking instructions. Flavorful dipping sauces that are low in both fat and sodium are also provided to accompany your delicious spring rolls.

SPRING ROLL WRAPPERS

There are two types of spring roll wrappers. One is a fresh noodle made from white flour and water. It is flat and square in shape. Traditionally, spring rolls made with this type of wrapper are deep-fried, but in this book they are steamed.

Rice paper wrappers, the second type used for spring rolls, are made from rice flour and water. Translucent and delicate, these wrappers are sold dry and can be stored for many weeks in the pantry. They must be soaked in warm water for a few seconds before they are filled. When using rice paper wrappers, be sure to soak them just before filling them and fill only one at a time. Unlike spring rolls made with fresh wrappers, those made with rice paper wrappers can be eaten as is, without further cooking. They can also be broiled, which makes them delightfully crisp.

MAKING SPRING ROLLS

Making spring rolls is both fun and easy. Simply follow the steps in Figure 3.1 for perfect spring rolls every time.

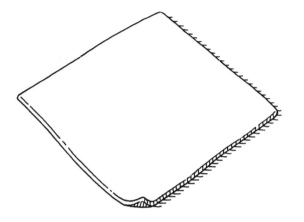

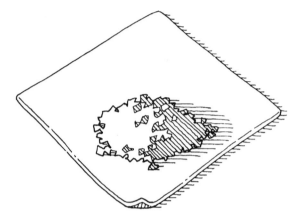

1. Place the wrapper on a clean flat surface with one corner pointing toward you.

2. Place about 2 tablespoons of filling in an even horizontal mound just below the center of the wrapper. (Don't overstuff.)

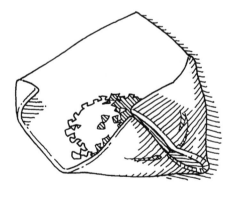

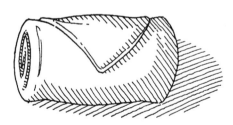

3. Fold the bottom corner over the filling, followed by the right and left corners.

4. Starting at the bottom, tightly roll up the filling in the wrapper. Moisten the top edges of the wrapper and press against the filled roll to seal.

Figure 3.1.   Making Spring Rolls

COOKING SPRING ROLLS

Steaming and broiling are the two basic methods for cooking spring rolls. The exception is for some rolls with precooked fillings that are made with rice paper wrappers. These require no cooking at all.

Steaming Method

To steam spring rolls, simply place them on a lightly oiled steamer set over boiling water. Steam the rolls about 15 to 20 minutes or until the wrappers are soft and translucent. Make sure the rolls are not touching as they cook.

Instead of using oil, you can line the steamer with green cabbage leaves and place the rolls on top. Add an additional 3 to 5 minutes steaming time when using this method.

Broiling Method

To broil spring rolls, lightly coat a nonstick baking sheet with cooking spray. Place the rolls on the sheet, leaving a little space between them. Lightly spray the rolls with the cooking spray. Broil the rolls for 10 to 15 minutes until they are golden brown. Using a spatula, turn the rolls over and broil another 10 minutes.

Dumplings

Like the Christmas holiday celebrated in the West, the Chinese New Year is a time for families to gather and celebrate. Traditionally, family members surround the dinner table and take part in making dumplings while reminiscing about the year that has passed and anticipating the year to come. The dumpling is as much a part of the Chinese New Year as turkey is to an American Thanksgiving.

Dumplings were first served thousands of years ago. Over time, variations of these plump meat- or vegetable-filled treats have evolved. The variety of dumpling fillings is endless. Feel free to be creative. Generally, I use extra-lean ground meat or low-fat tofu as the filling's base, then I add minced cabbage, carrots, and other fresh vegetables. Depending on your taste, you can add any one of a number of seasonings to make a filling that ranges from mild and plain to sweet and sour to hot and spicy. It's up to you. Once filled and sealed, dumplings can be steamed, boiled, or pan-fried.

Perfect party fare, dumplings are also appealing to the busy cook. They can be prepared in large quantities, frozen and stored for many weeks, and then cooked in just a few minutes.

DUMPLING WRAPPERS

Like spring roll wrappers, dumpling wrappers are basically fresh noodles made primarily of white flour and water. (As some commercial wrappers are made with eggs, be sure to read labels.) Most grocery stores, health food stores, and Asian markets stock packages of fresh dumpling wrappers in their produce or refrigerated foods sections. The wrappers can be frozen until needed.

Dumpling wrappers are square or circular. The square-shaped ones are called wonton wrappers, while those that are circular in shape are generally labeled shanghai or gyoza (guh-yo-za) dumpling skins. These circular wrappers also vary in thickness. Although you can use either wrapper to make dumplings, I have found that the thicker circular skins are better for boiled dumplings, while the thinner circular skins are good for those that are pan-fried. The square wonton skins are ideal for steamed dumplings.

MAKING DUMPLINGS

The main goal when preparing dumplings is to keep the wrapper and the filling from separating! Always keep the wrappers chilled until you have prepared the filling and are ready to start cooking. Place the dumplings on a lightly floured plate to keep them from sticking until you are ready to cook them.

Making dumplings is simple. Figure 3.2 (below) provides the steps for making dumplings with circular wrappers, while Figure 3.3 illustrates how to use square wrappers.

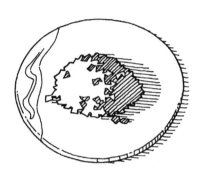 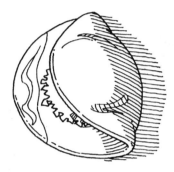 

1. Dip one edge of the wrapper in water. Place a heaping teaspoon of filling in the center.

2. Fold the wrapper in half to form a half circle.

3. Pinch the edges together to seal.

Figure 3.2. Making Dumplings with Circular (Gyoza) Wrappers

 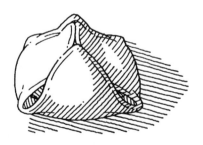 

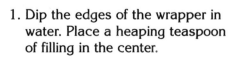

1. Dip the edges of the wrapper in water. Place a heaping teaspoon of filling in the center.

2. Bring up the four corners over the filling.

3. Pinch the edges together to seal.

Figure 3.3. Making Dumplings with Square (Wonton) Wrappers

COOKING DUMPLINGS

Steaming, boiling, and pan-frying are the three basic methods for cooking dumplings.

Steaming Method

Steamed dumplings—a specialty of Beijing — traditionally are cooked in a bamboo steamer. You can, however, use a metal steamer instead. Metal steamers are usually heavily oiled before the dumplings are placed on top and then set over boiling water. Instead of using oil, you can line the steamer with cabbage leaves. You can also cut thin cross-sections of carrot and place a piece under each dumpling. Not only will this prevent the dumplings from sticking to the steamer, you can enjoy the carrots as well. Allow at least one inch of space between the steamer and the boiling water.

In order for the dumplings to cook evenly, a proper water level below the steamer must be maintained. Therefore, always have water boiling, say in a teapot, while you are steaming the dumplings. If the water level gets too low, simply add more boiling water to the pot. When the dumpling skins become soft and translucent, usually about 10 minutes, you can remove them from the steamer and enjoy them along with your favorite dipping sauce.

Boiling Method

Boiled dumplings, which are very popular in North China, especially during the long, cold winters, are quick and easy to cook. Use the following procedure when boiling dumplings. (The water measurements are appropriate for the dumpling recipes in this book.)

Bring seven cups of water to a boil in a large pot, then add the dumplings one at a time. As soon as the water comes to a second boil, add a quarter cup of cold water (this step

is the key to successfully cooked boiled dumplings). Bring the water to another boil and cook the dumplings for about a minute. Add another half cup of cold water, bring to a final boil, and remove the dumplings with a slotted spoon. (For high altitude cooking or for cooking dumplings with thick wrappers, you may have to add more cold water and bring to another boil.)

Pan-Frying Method

Traditional pan-fried dumplings are first fried in oil then steamed with water. Too oily. My desire to pan-fry dumplings without all the oil caused me to experiment. After much kitchen testing, I came up with a nearly fat-free pan-frying method that results in dumplings that are absolutely delicious—crisp and light outside, and moist and juicy inside! As an added bonus, cleanup is easy.

First, coat a 14-inch nonstick frying pan (or two 10-inch frying pans) with cooking spray. Place the dumplings in a winding circle in the frying pan, leaving a little space between each. Cover and cook over medium-high heat until the dumplings begin to puff up and their bottoms turn light brown (about three to five minutes). Add water (1 cup for a 10-inch pan, $1^1/2$ cups for a 14-inch pan) and reduce the heat to medium-low. Cover and simmer the dumplings until most of the water cooks off (about seven to ten minutes). Remove the dumplings and serve with dipping sauce.

Dipping Sauces

Along with each of the spring roll and dumpling recipes found in this chapter, specific dipping sauces have been recommended. However, don't limit yourself to those suggested. Feel free to try any of the sauces. They are all perfect accompaniments for a variety of spring rolls and dumplings.

Top Left: Spinach with Sesame Seeds (page 94)
Top Right: Party Rice (page 64)
Bottom: Lemony Chicken Salad (page 104)

Spring Rolls

Steamed Beef Spring Rolls

Yield: 12 rolls

12 spring roll wrappers

FILLING

8 ounces extra-lean ground beef

1 cup bean sprouts

1/2 cup thinly sliced bamboo shoots

6 shiitake mushroom caps, sliced (if using dried variety, *see* hydrating instructions below)

2 teaspoons minced fresh ginger

1/2 teaspoon commercial or Home-made Chili Paste (page 13)

1/2 teaspoon low-sodium soy sauce

1/2 teaspoon ground black pepper

1/2 teaspoon five-spice powder

1. Mix the filling ingredients together in a large bowl. Let sit for 5 minutes.

2. Follow the instructions in Figure 3.1 (page 32) to form spring rolls.

3. Place the rolls on a lightly oiled steamer (or a steamer lined with green cabbage leaves*) set over boiling water. Do not let the rolls touch.

4. Steam the rolls until the wrappers are soft and translucent (15 to 20 minutes).

5. Serve with Hot Dipping Sauce (page 56).

* If using cabbage leaves, allow an extra 3 to 5 minutes steaming time.

NUTRITIONAL FACTS (PER ROLL)

Calories: 46 Carbohydrates: 2.9 g Cholesterol: 10 mg
Fat: 2.5 g Fiber: 0.6 g Protein: 3.2 g Sodium: 27 mg

Hydrating Dried Mushrooms

Many mushroom varieties come in both fresh and dried forms. One such mushroom, the shiitake, is used in many recipes in this book. To hydrate dried mushrooms, do the following:

1. Soak the mushrooms in hot water until they soften. (Soaking time varies with type and size.)

2. Rinse the gills (the underside) under running water to clean them of any dirt or sand.

3. Squeeze the mushrooms in your fist to thoroughly wring out the water.

4. Remove and discard any tough woody stems.

The hydrated mushrooms can now be sliced, minced, chopped, or used in their entirety. Dried mushrooms will keep indefinitely in an airtight container or in the freezer.

Broiled Curried Chicken Spring Rolls

Yield: *12 rolls*

12 rice paper wrappers

FILLING

4 ounces extra-lean ground chicken

2 green onions, minced

1 carrot, minced

1 cup minced cabbage

1 teaspoon minced fresh ginger

1 teaspoon curry powder

¼ cup low-sodium fat-free chicken broth

2 tablespoons cornstarch

1. Mix all of the filling ingredients, except the broth and cornstarch, together in a large bowl. Dissolve the cornstarch in the broth and add to the mixture.

2. Fill a bowl with warm water. Place one of the wrappers in the water and soak for 10 to 15 seconds until soft. Transfer to a dry flat surface.

3. Follow instructions in Figure 3.1 (page 32) to form the spring roll. Repeat with the remaining wrappers and filling.

4. Lightly coat a large nonstick baking sheet with cooking spray. Place the rolls on the sheet, leaving a little space between them. Lightly coat the rolls with cooking spray.

5. Broil the rolls until they are golden brown (10 to 15 minutes). Using a spatula, turn the rolls over and continue to broil another 10 minutes.

6. Serve with Sweet-and-Hot Dipping Sauce (page 57).

NUTRITIONAL FACTS (PER ROLL)

Calories: **48** Carbohydrates: **8.4 g** Cholesterol: **3 mg**
Fat: **0.1 g** Fiber: **0.1 g** Protein: **2.3 g** Sodium: **35 mg**

Broiled Vegetable Spring Rolls

Yield: 12 rolls

12 rice paper wrappers

FILLING

1 cup bean sprouts

1/2 cup thinly sliced green pepper

1/2 cup thinly sliced Napa cabbage

1/2 cup bamboo shoots

12 sprigs fresh cilantro, finely chopped

1 teaspoon low-sodium soy sauce

1/2 teaspoon chili pepper flakes

1/4 teaspoon ground black pepper

1 teaspoon cornstarch

1. Mix all of the filling ingredients, except the cornstarch, in a large bowl. Dissolve the cornstarch in a teaspoon of water and add to the mixture. Refrigerate 30 minutes.

2. Fill a bowl with warm water. Place one of the wrappers in the water and soak about 10 to 15 seconds until soft. Transfer to a dry flat surface.

3. Follow instructions in Figure 3.1 (page 32) to form the spring roll. Repeat with the remaining wrappers and filling.

4. Lightly coat a large nonstick baking sheet with cooking spray. Place the rolls on the sheet, leaving a little space between them. Lightly coat the rolls with cooking spray.

5. Broil the rolls until they are golden brown (10 to 15 minutes). Using a spatula, turn the rolls over and continue to broil another 10 minutes.

6. Serve with Hot Dipping Sauce (page 56).

NUTRITIONAL FACTS (PER ROLL)

Calories: 41 Carbohydrates: 8.3 g Cholesterol: 0 mg
Fat: 0.1 g Fiber: 0.4 g Protein: 1.4 g Sodium: 42 mg

Foochow Dishes

Hailing from the province of Fukien, which runs along China's southern coast, are the famous Foochow dishes. Outstanding seafood and mushroom creations, as well as high-quality teas come from this region. Foochow dishes are characteristically soupy and light, and seasoned primarily with soy sauce. Occasionally, spicy red fermented bean sauce is used. Some of the specialty foods from this region include seaweed soups, rice noodles, spring rolls, and paper-thin pancakes.

Many of the soups presented in Chapter 2, such as Fish Onion and Green Tea and Beef are reflective of the Fukien region. Other low-fat versions of Foochow-style dishes include Scallops with Orange Peel on page 123 and Broiled Vegetable Spring Rolls, above.

Crabmeat Spring Rolls

Yield: *12 rolls*

12 rice paper wrappers

FILLING

8 ounces crabmeat, finely chopped*

16 ounces bean sprouts

4 sprigs fresh cilantro, minced

2 green onions, minced

1 teaspoon minced fresh ginger

1/2 teaspoon sesame oil

1/4 teaspoon five-spice powder

* Can use artificial variety.

1. In a large saucepan, bring 4 cups of water to a boil. Add the crabmeat and bean sprouts and cook for 2 minutes. Drain and transfer to a large bowl.

2. Add the remaining filling ingredients and mix well.

3. Fill a bowl with warm water. Place one of the wrappers in the water and soak for 10 to 15 seconds until soft. Transfer to a dry flat surface.

4. Follow instructions in Figure 3.1 (page 32) to form the spring roll. Repeat with remaining wrappers and filling.

5. As these rolls need no further cooking, you can serve them immediately. They are delicious with Hot Dipping Sauce (page 56).

NUTRITIONAL FACTS (PER ROLL)

Calories: 54 Carbohydrates: 8.1 g Cholesterol: 11 mg
Fat: 0.4 g Fiber: 0.5 g Protein: 4.1 g Sodium: 83 mg

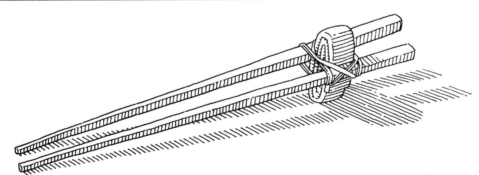

Using Chopsticks the Easy Way

Have you ever tried to eat with chopsticks but found that you lacked the dexterity (or patience) to hold them the traditional way? No problem. Simply do the following: fold up a small piece of paper or cardboard (a matchbook cover is good) and place it between two chopsticks as shown in the figure above. Band the sticks together with a rubber band and you are ready. For instructions on how to hold chopsticks the traditional way, see the inset on page 49.

Steamed Fish Spring Rolls

1. Combine the marinade ingredients in a large bowl. Add the fish and marinate for 15 minutes.

2. Add the remaining filling ingredients to the bowl and mix together with the fish.

3. Follow the instructions in Figure 3.1 (page 32) to form the spring rolls.

4. Place the rolls on a lightly oiled steamer (or a steamer lined with green cabbage leaves*) set over boiling water. Do not let the rolls touch. Steam the rolls until the wrappers are soft and translucent (15 to 20 minutes).

5. Serve with Ginger-and-Vinegar Dipping Sauce (page 57).

* If using cabbage leaves, allow additional 3 to 5 minutes steaming time.

NUTRITIONAL FACTS (PER ROLL)
Calories: 57 Carbohydrates: 8.6 g Cholesterol: 6 mg
Fat: 0.4 g Fiber: 0.5 g Protein: 4.1 g Sodium: 48 mg

Yield: 12 rolls

12 spring roll wrappers

MARINADE

1/2 teaspoon fresh lime juice

1/2 teaspoon rice wine

1/8 teaspoon rice vinegar

1 teaspoon minced fresh garlic

1/2 teaspoon minced fresh ginger

FILLING

8 ounces sole fillet, minced

8 ounces bean sprouts

1 large white onion, minced

4 green onions, minced

1 teaspoon five-spice powder

1/2 teaspoon sesame oil

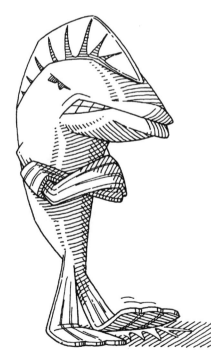

Broiled Spicy Tofu Spring Rolls

Yield: 12 rolls

12 rice paper wrappers

FILLING

16 ounces firm low-fat tofu,
  finely crumbled

6 shiitake mushroom caps,
  minced (if using dried variety,
  see hydrating instructions on
  page 37)

2 teaspoons minced fresh garlic

1 teaspoon low-sodium soy sauce

1 teaspoon sesame oil

½ teaspoon commercial or Home-
  made Chili Paste (page 13)

1 green onion, minced

1. Mix the filling ingredients together in a large bowl.

2. Fill a bowl with warm water. Place one of the wrappers in the water and soak for 10 to 15 seconds until soft. Transfer to a dry flat surface.

3. Follow instructions in Figure 3.1 (page 32) to form the spring roll. Repeat with the remaining wrappers and filling.

4. Lightly coat a large nonstick baking sheet with cooking spray. Place the rolls on the sheet, leaving a little space between them. Lightly coat the rolls with cooking spray.

5. Broil the rolls until they are golden brown (10 to 15 minutes). Using a spatula, turn the rolls over and continue to broil another 10 minutes.

6. Serve with Ginger-and-Vinegar Dipping Sauce (page 57).

NUTRITIONAL FACTS (PER ROLL)

Calories: 61 Carbohydrates: 8.8 g Cholesterol: 0 mg
Fat: 0.8 g Fiber: 0.3 g Protein: 3.9 g Sodium: 77 mg

Celebrating
Chinese New Year

The date of the Chinese New Year is determined by the lunar calendar. Usually falling in late January or early February, the New Year celebration begins on the day of the year's first new moon and ends fifteen days later with the Lantern Festival on the night of the year's first full moon.

Twelve animals represent each new year in a sequence of twelve years. Five cycles of twelve years make up one complete cycle. Each cycle starts with the rat and follows with the ox, tiger, rabbit, dragon, snake, horse, ram, monkey, rooster, dog, and pig. The significance of their sequence and how these particular animals were chosen is the source of many legends. One popular legend claims that before Buddha departed from Earth, he invited all of the animals to join him in a celebration, and these twelve creatures were the only ones to come. As a token of his gratitude, he named a year after each animal in the order of their arrival.

New Year's Eve is the most important holiday for a Chinese family. All of the family members gather together and enjoy a great feast. Traditional foods are served and symbolic rites are performed. Noodles, which represent long life, are always part of the celebration banquet. A chicken is prepared and served, symbolizing family unity and wealth. And **yu**, a whole fish, is traditionally served near the meal's end, where it is enjoyed but not completely eaten. The leftover fish signifies that the family will not go hungry—that there is more for the next year. Dumplings, rice, and vegetables are also served. Every feast traditionally ends with **nin go** or New Year's cake. Considered the most important dish, nin go is believed to bring luck and good fortune to the family for the entire year.

After the New Year's Eve meal, as a symbol of respect, young children ceremoniously bow to their elders, who, in turn, hand the children small red bags called **liese**, which contain goodluck money. On New Year's Day, it is important for the children to wear new clothes. Not only does this symbolize a fresh start, it is also meant to confuse any evil spirits, who won't recognize the children in their new clothes.

Why not prepare your own Chinese-style New Year's Eve feast this year? Instead of the usual dinner, serve your family and friends the following meal:

After a fifteen-day celebration, the New Year festivities end with the Lantern Festival. More information on this special holiday is found on page 86.

Vegetable Spring Rolls

Yield: *12 rolls*

12 rice paper wrappers

FILLING

16 ounces snow peas, thinly sliced

1 large red bell pepper, cut
  into thin strips

1/2 cup minced fresh basil leaves

2 sprigs fresh cilantro, minced

1 green onion, minced

1 teaspoon commercial or Home-
  made Chili Paste (page 13)

1/2 teaspoon minced fresh garlic

1/4 teaspoon Eden Foods sesame
  shake, or chopped sesame seeds

1. In a medium saucepan, bring 4 cups of water to a boil. Add the snow peas and bell pepper and cook for 2 minutes. Drain and rinse with cold water. Transfer to a large bowl.

2. Add the remaining filling ingredients to the bowl and mix well.

3. Fill a bowl with warm water. Place one of the wrappers in the water and soak for 10 to 15 seconds until soft. Transfer to a dry flat surface.

4. Follow instructions in Figure 3.1 (page 32) to form the spring roll. Repeat with the remaining wrappers and filling.

5. As these rolls need no further cooking, you can serve them immediately. Try them with Sweet-and-Hot Dipping Sauce (page 57).

NUTRITIONAL FACTS (PER ROLL)

Calories: 54 Carbohydrates: 10.4 g Cholesterol: 0 mg
Fat: 0.1 g Fiber: 1.5 g Protein: 2 g Sodium: 42 mg

Dumplings

Steamed Vegetarian Dumplings

1. Mix the filling ingredients together in a large bowl.

2. Follow the instructions in Figure 3.3 (page 34) to form the dumplings.

3. Set the carrot slices on the steamer and place a dumpling on each (the carrots will keep the dumplings from sticking to the steamer). Be sure to leave a little space between the dumplings to prevent them from sticking to each other.

4. Set the steamer in a pot over boiling water (make sure the water is not touching the dumplings). Cover and steam the dumplings until they are soft and translucent (7 to 10 minutes). Allow the dumplings to cool for a minute or two before removing them from the steamer.

5. Serve with Soy-Vinegar Dipping Sauce (page 56).

NUTRITIONAL FACTS (PER DUMPLING)

Calories: 44 Carbohydrates: 8.8 g Cholesterol: 0 mg
Fat: 0.1 g Fiber: 0.5 g Protein: 1.3 g Sodium: 46 mg

Yield: *40 dumplings*

40 wonton (square) wrappers

40 thin circular carrot slices

FILLING

8 shiitake mushroom caps, minced (if using dried variety, *see* hydrating instructions on page 37)

2 green onions, minced

3 cups finely chopped green cabbage

1 cup finely chopped carrots

2 teaspoons minced fresh ginger

1/4 cup low-sodium fat-free vegetable broth

2 tablespoons low-sodium soy sauce

1 tablespoon sesame oil

slightly bitter

Steamed Beef-and-Vegetable Dumplings

Yield: 40 dumplings

40 wonton (square) wrappers

40 thin circular carrot slices

FILLING

8 ounces extra-lean ground beef

2 cups minced carrots

2 cups minced white onions

1 cup minced green onion

2 teaspoons fresh lemon juice

1½ teaspoons hot mustard sauce

1 teaspoon commercial or Home-
   made Chili Paste (page 13)

1 teaspoon sesame oil

1. Mix the filling ingredients together in a large bowl.

2. Follow the instructions in Figure 3.3 (page 34) to form the dumplings.

3. Set the carrot slices on the steamer and place a dumpling on each (the carrots will keep the dumplings from sticking to the steamer). Be sure to leave a little space between the dumplings to prevent them from sticking to each other.

4. Set the steamer in a pot over boiling water (make sure the water is not touching the dumplings). Cover and steam the dumplings until they are soft and translucent (about 15 minutes). Allow the dumplings to cool for a minute or two before removing them from the steamer.

5. Serve with Soy-Vinegar Dipping Sauce (page 56).

NUTRITIONAL FACTS (PER DUMPLING)
Calories: 53 Carbohydrates: 8.7 g Cholesterol: 3 mg
Fat: 0.9 g Fiber: 0.4 g Protein: 2 g Sodium: 43 mg

Boiled Turkey-and-Vegetable Dumplings

Yield: 40 dumplings

40 round dumpling wrappers

FILLING

8 ounces extra-lean ground turkey

½ cup finely chopped water
   chestnuts

¼ low-sodium fat-free chicken broth

4 cloves garlic, crushed

3 green onions, minced

3 springs fresh cilantro, minced

1 tablespoon honey mustard

½ teaspoon ground white pepper

1. Mix the filling ingredients together in a large bowl.

2. Follow the instructions in Figure 3.2 (page 34) to form the dumplings.

3. In a large pot, bring 7 cups of water to a boil. Place the dumplings one at a time in the pot and bring the water to a second boil. Immediately add ¼ cup cold water to the pot and bring to another boil. Cook the dumplings for about a minute, add another ½ cup cold water, and bring to a final boil. Remove the dumplings with a slotted spoon.

4. Serve with Chili-and-Garlic Dipping Sauce (page 55).

NUTRITIONAL FACTS (PER DUMPLING)
Calories: 43 Carbohydrates: 7.7 g Cholesterol: 2 mg
Fat: 0.1 g Fiber: 0.1 g Protein: 2.1 g Sodium: 41 mg

Steamed Shrimp Dumplings

1. Mix all of the filling ingredients, except the wine and corn-starch, together in a large bowl. Dissolve the cornstarch in the wine and add to the mixture.

2. Follow the instructions in Figure 3.3 (page 34) to form the dumplings.

3. Set the carrot slices on the steamer and place a dumpling on each (the carrots will keep the dumplings from sticking to the steamer). Be sure to leave a little space between the dumplings to prevent them from sticking to each other.

4. Set the steamer in a pot over boiling water (make sure the water is not touching the dumplings). Cover and steam the dumplings until they are soft and translucent (7 to 10 min-utes). Allow the dumplings to cool for a minute or two before removing them from the steamer.

5. Serve with Chili-and-Garlic Dipping Sauce (page 55).

Yield: 40 dumplings

40 wonton (square) wrappers

40 thin circular carrot slices

FILLING

8 ounces fresh shrimp, deveined and cut into very small pieces

$1/2$ cup finely minced leeks

1 teaspoon minced fresh ginger

1 teaspoon Eden Foods sesame shake, or chopped sesame seeds

1 teaspoon ground white pepper

1 tablespoon cooking wine

1 teaspoon cornstarch

NUTRITIONAL FACTS (PER DUMPLING)

Calories: 40 Carbohydrates: 7.7 g Cholesterol: 9 mg
Fat: 0.1 g Fiber: 0.2 g Protein: 2.2 g Sodium: 47 mg

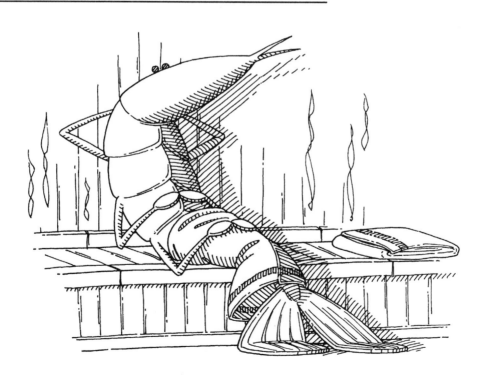

Steamed Fish Dumplings

Yield: 40 dumplings

40 wonton (square) wrappers

40 thin circular carrot slices

FILLING

8 ounces fillet of sole, sea bass, or other white fish, cut into 3-inch pieces

1 cup coarsely chopped white onion

2 tablespoons Rice Dream beverage, or reduced-fat soymilk

2 tablespoons cornstarch

2 tablespoons cooking wine

1 teaspoon minced fresh ginger

1 teaspoon five-spice powder

1. Process the fish, onion, and Rice Dream in a blender or food processor until smooth. Transfer the mixture to a large bowl. Dissolve the cornstarch in the wine and add it to the mixture along with the ginger and five-spice powder.

2. Follow the instructions in Figure 3.3 (page 34) to form the dumplings.

3. Set the carrot slices on the steamer and place a dumpling on each (the carrots will keep the dumplings from sticking to the steamer). Be sure to leave a little space between the dumplings to prevent them from sticking to each other.

4. Set the steamer in a pot over boiling water (make sure the water is not touching the dumplings). Cover and steam the dumplings until they are soft and translucent (7 to 10 minutes). Allow the dumplings to cool for a minute or two before removing them from the steamer.

5. Serve with Mustard Dipping Sauce (page 56).

NUTRITIONAL FACTS (PER DUMPLING)

Calories: 46 Carbohydrates: 8.3 g Cholesterol: 3 mg
Fat: 0.1 g Fiber: 0.2 g Protein: 2.2 g Sodium: 42 mg

Pan-Fried Curried Turkey Dumplings

1. Mix the filling ingredients together in a large bowl.

2. Follow the instructions in Figure 3.2 (page 34) to form the dumplings.

3. Lightly coat a 14-inch nonstick frying pan (or two 10-inch frying pans) with cooking spray. Place the dumplings in a winding circle in the pan, leaving a little space between each. Cover and cook over medium-high heat until the dumplings begin to puff up and their bottoms turn light brown (3 to 5 minutes).

4. Add 1¹/₂ cups of water to the pan (or 1 cup in each 10-inch pan), and reduce the heat to medium-low. Cover and simmer the dumplings until most of the water cooks off (7 to 10 minutes).

5. Serve with Chili-and-Garlic Dipping Sauce (page 55) or Mustard Dipping Sauce (page 56).

Yield: *40 dumplings*

40 round dumpling wrappers
(thin)

FILLING

8 ounces extra-lean ground turkey

1 cup minced white onion

3 cloves garlic, crushed

1¹/₂ teaspoons red curry paste

1 teaspoon minced fresh ginger

1 egg white

NUTRITIONAL FACTS (PER DUMPLING)

Calories: 43 Carbohydrates: 7.4 g Cholesterol: 3 mg
Fat: 0.1 g Fiber: 0.1 g Protein: 2.5 g Sodium: 35 mg

Using Chopsticks the Traditional Way

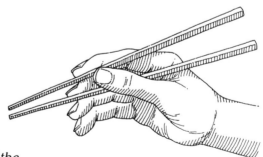

1. Place one chopstick between the tips of the middle finger and the ring finger. Use your thumb to brace the chopstick. (Beginners should hold the chopsticks close to the bottom.)

2. Place the second chopstick between your thumb tip and the tip of your index finger (as you would hold a pencil). Hold it lightly so you can move it up and down against the other chopstick.

3. When you are ready to pick up food, separate the tips of the chopsticks by moving your index finger upward. Pinch the food between the sticks by moving your index finger downward and clamping both tips onto the food.

4. Pop the food into your mouth.

Pan-Fried Tofu Dumplings

Yield: 40 dumplings

40 round dumpling wrappers
(thin)

FILLING

8 ounces soft low-fat tofu

10 shiitake mushroom caps, minced
(if using dried variety, *see* hydrating instructions on page 37)

4 garlic cloves, crushed

3 green onions, minced

1/4 cup low-sodium fat-free
vegetable broth

1 tablespoon sweet-and-sour sauce

1. Mash the tofu in a large bowl. Add the remaining filling
ingredients and mix well.

2. Follow instructions in Figure 3.2 (page 34) to form dumplings.

3. Lightly coat a 14-inch nonstick frying pan (or two 10-inch
frying pans) with cooking spray. Place the dumplings in a winding circle in the pan, leaving a little space between each. Cover
and cook over medium-high heat until the dumplings begin to
puff up and their bottoms turn light brown (3 to 5 minutes).

4. Add $1^1/2$ cups of water to the pan (or 1 cup in each 10-inch
pan), and reduce the heat to medium-low. Cover and simmer the
dumplings until most of the water cooks off (7 to 10 minutes).

5. Serve with Chili-and-Garlic Dipping Sauce (page 55).

NUTRITIONAL FACTS (PER DUMPLING)
Calories: 43 Carbohydrates: 8.3 g Cholesterol: 0 mg
Fat: 0.2 g Fiber: 0.2 g Protein: 1.4 g Sodium: 33 mg

Pan-Fried Cheese-and-Spinach Dumplings

Yield: 40 dumplings

40 round dumpling wrappers
(thin)

FILLING

8 ounces fat-free cream cheese,
softened to room temperature

3 cups chopped fresh spinach

1 teaspoon sweet-and-hot mustard
sauce

1. Mix the filling ingredients together in a medium bowl.
Cover and refrigerate for 1 hour.

2. Follow instructions in Figure 3.2 (page 34) to form dumplings.

3. Lightly coat a 14-inch nonstick frying pan (or two 10-inch
frying pans) with cooking spray. Place the dumplings in a winding circle in the pan, leaving a little space between each. Cover
and cook over medium-high heat until the dumplings begin to
puff up and their bottoms turn light brown (3 to 5 minutes).

4. Add $1^1/2$ cups of water to the pan (or 1 cup in each 10-inch
pan), and reduce the heat to medium-low. Cover and simmer the
dumplings until most of the water cooks off (7 to 10 minutes).

5. Serve with Soy-Vinegar Dipping Sauce (page 56).

NUTRITIONAL FACTS (PER DUMPLING)
Calories: 41 Carbohydrates: 7.4 g Cholesterol: 1 mg
Fat: 0 g Fiber: 0.1 g Protein: 1.9 g Sodium: 68 mg

Boiled Pork-and-Vegetable Dumplings

1. Mix the filling ingredients together in a large bowl.

2. Follow the instructions in Figure 3.2 (page 34) to form the dumplings.

3. In a large pot, bring 7 cups of water to a boil. Place the dumplings one at a time in the pot and bring the water to a second boil. Immediately add $^1/_4$ cup cold water to the pot and bring to another boil. Cook the dumplings for about a minute, add another $^1/_2$ cup cold water, and bring to a final boil. Remove the dumplings with a slotted spoon.

4. Serve with Soy-Vinegar Dipping Sauce (page 56).

NUTRITIONAL FACTS (PER DUMPLING)

Calories: 50 Carbohydrates: 7.5 g Cholesterol: 3 mg
Fat: 0.9 g Fiber: 0.2 g Protein: 1.9 g Sodium: 37 mg

Yield: 40 dumplings

40 round dumpling wrappers (thick)

FILLING

8 ounces extra-lean ground pork

3 cups minced bok choy (squeeze out excess water)

5 shiitake mushroom caps, minced (if using dried variety, *see* hydrating instructions on page 37)

$^1/_4$ cup low-sodium fat-free chicken broth

2 tablespoons minced fresh ginger

1 teaspoon minced fresh garlic

1 teaspoon five-spice powder

1 teaspoon Eden Foods sesame shake, or chopped sesame seeds

Steamed Crabmeat Dumplings

Yield: 40 dumplings

40 wonton (square) wrappers

40 thin circular carrot slices

FILLING

8 ounces crabmeat, minced*

1/2 cup minced carrots

3 sprigs fresh cilantro, minced

1 teaspoon cooking wine

1 teaspoon minced fresh ginger

1 teaspoon five-spice powder

* Can use artificial variety.

1. Mix the filling ingredients together in a large bowl.

2. Follow the instructions in Figure 3.3 (page 34) to form the dumplings.

3. Set the carrot slices on the steamer and place a dumpling on each (the carrots will keep the dumplings from sticking to the steamer). Be sure to leave a little space between the dumplings to prevent them from sticking to each other.

4. Set the steamer in a pot over boiling water (make sure the water is not touching the dumplings). Cover and steam the dumplings until they are soft and translucent (7 to 10 minutes). Allow the dumplings to cool for a minute or two before removing them from the steamer.

5. Serve with Chili-and-Garlic Dipping Sauce (page 55).

NUTRITIONAL FACTS (PER DUMPLING)

Calories: 44 Carbohydrates: 7.6 g Cholesterol: 6 mg
Fat: 0.1 g Fiber: 0.2 g Protein: 2.2 g Sodium: 49 mg

Boiled Potato-and-Vegetable Dumplings

Yield: 40 dumplings

40 round dumpling wrappers (thick)

FILLING

1 1/2 cups mashed potatoes

4 green onions, minced

2 tablespoons Arrowhead Mills easy-spreading peanut butter

2 tablespoons chopped fresh mint

1/2 teaspoon commercial or Homemade Chili Paste (page 13)

1/2 teaspoon Eden Foods sesame shake, or chopped sesame seeds

1/8 teaspoon ground black pepper

1. Mix all the filling ingredients together in a large bowl.

2. Follow the instructions in Figure 3.2 (page 34) to form the dumplings.

3. In a large pot, bring 7 cups of water to a boil. Place the dumplings one at a time in the pot and bring the water to a second boil. Immediately add 1/4 cup cold water to the pot and bring to another boil. Cook the dumplings for about a minute, add another 1/2 cup cold water, and bring to a final boil. Remove the dumplings with a slotted spoon.

4. Serve with Mustard Dipping Sauce (page 56).

NUTRITIONAL FACTS (PER DUMPLING)

Calories: 47 Carbohydrates: 8.9 g Cholesterol: 0 mg
Fat: 0.3 g Fiber: 0.2 g Protein: 1.4 g Sodium: 40 mg

Pan-Fried Ginger-and-Scallop Dumplings

1. Mix the filling ingredients together in a large bowl.

2. Follow the instructions in Figure 3.2 (page 34) to form the dumplings.

3. Lightly coat a 14-inch nonstick frying pan (or two 10-inch frying pans) with cooking spray. Place the dumplings in a winding circle in the pan, leaving a little space between each. Cover and cook over medium-high heat until the dumplings begin to puff up and their bottoms turn light brown (3 to 5 minutes).

4. Add $1^{1}/_{2}$ cups of water to the pan (or 1 cup in each 10-inch pan), and reduce the heat to medium-low. Cover and simmer the dumplings until most of the water cooks off (7 to 10 minutes).

5. Serve with Soy-Vinegar Dipping Sauce (page 55).

Yield: 40 dumplings

40 round dumpling wrappers (thin)

FILLING

8 ounces fresh scallops, cut into very small pieces

$1/4$ cup finely chopped white mushrooms

2 cloves garlic, crushed

2 tablespoons minced fresh ginger

1 tablespoon fresh lemon juice

1 teaspoon Eden Foods sesame shake, or chopped sesame seeds

$1/4$ teaspoon chili pepper flakes

NUTRITIONAL FACTS (PER DUMPLING)

Calories: 42 Carbohydrates: 7.2 g Cholesterol: 2 mg
Fat: 0.1 g Fiber: 0 g Protein: 2 g Sodium: 40 mg

Boiled Beef-and-Vegetable Dumplings

1. Mix the filling ingredients together in a large bowl.

2. Follow the instructions in Figure 3.2 (page 34) to form the dumplings.

3. In a large pot, bring 7 cups of water to a boil. Place the dumplings one at a time in the pot and bring the water to a second boil. Immediately add $1/4$ cup cold water to the pot and bring to another boil. Cook the dumplings for about a minute, add another $1/2$ cup cold water, and bring to a final boil. Remove the dumplings with a slotted spoon.

4. Serve with Five-Spice Dipping Sauce (page 55).

Yield: 40 dumplings

40 round dumpling wrappers (thick)

FILLING

8 ounces extra-lean ground beef

4 cups finely chopped green cabbage (squeeze out excess water)

4 cloves garlic, crushed

3 springs fresh cilantro, minced

$1/4$ cup low-sodium fat-free beef broth

2 teaspoons sweet-and-hot mustard sauce

NUTRITIONAL FACTS (PER DUMPLING)

Calories: 48 Carbohydrates: 7.6 g Cholesterol: 3 mg
Fat: 0.7 g Fiber: 0.2 g Protein: 1.9 g Sodium: 37 mg

Sauces

Chili-and-Garlic Dipping Sauce

1. Mix all of the ingredients together in a small bowl. Refrigerate at least 30 minutes before serving.

2. To store, place in a tightly sealed container and refrigerate.

Yield: $^1/_2$ cup

$^1/_4$ cup fresh lime juice

$1^1/_2$ tablespoons commercial or Homemade Chili Paste (page 13)

2 tablespoons cooking wine

5 cloves garlic, minced

NUTRITION FACTS (PER TABLESPOON)

Calories: 5 Carbohydrates: 1.9 g Cholesterol: 0 mg
Fat: 0 g Fiber: 0 g Protein: 0.2 Sodium: 88 mg

Five-Spice Dipping Sauce

1. Dissolve the five-spice powder in the Rice Dream, then stir in the sesame shake and serve.

2. To store, place in a tightly sealed container and refrigerate.

Yield: $^2/_3$ cup

$^1/_2$ cup + 1 tablespoon Rice Dream beverage, or reduced-fat soymilk

2 teaspoons five-spice powder

1 teaspoon Eden Foods sesame shake, or chopped sesame seeds

NUTRITIONAL FACTS (PER TABLESPOON)

Calories: 16 Carbohydrates: 3 g Cholesterol: 0 mg
Fat: 0 g Fiber: 0 g Protein: 0 g Sodium: 13 mg

Mustard Dipping Sauce

Yield: $^2/_3$ cup

$^1/_2$ cup Rice Dream beverage, or reduced-fat soymilk

2 tablespoons extra-hot mustard sauce

2 sprigs fresh cilantro, minced

1. Combine the Rice Dream and mustard in a small bowl. Serve garnished with cilantro.

2. To store, place in a tightly sealed container and refrigerate.

NUTRITIONAL FACTS (PER TABLESPOON)
Calories: 15 Carbohydrates: 2.7 g Cholesterol: 0 mg
Fat: 0.2 g Fiber: 0 g Protein: 0.1 g Sodium: 37 mg

Hot Dipping Sauce

Yield: $^1/_2$ cup

3 tablespoons low-sodium soy sauce

$^1/_4$ cup rice vinegar

1 teaspoon commercial or Home-made Chili Paste (page 13)

$^1/_2$ teaspoon sesame oil

4 cloves garlic, minced

1. Mix all of the ingredients together in a small bowl. Let stand at least 30 minutes before using.

2. To store, place in a tightly sealed container and refrigerate.

NUTRITIONAL FACTS (PER TABLESPOON)
Calories: 6 Carbohydrates: 1 g Cholesterol: 0 mg
Fat: 0.3 g Fiber: 0 g Protein: 0.3 g Sodium: 92 mg

Soy-Vinegar Dipping Sauce

Yield: $^3/_4$ cup

$^1/_2$ cup fresh lime juice

2 tablespoons rice vinegar

$1^1/_2$ tablespoons light miso paste

$^1/_2$ teaspoon sesame oil

1. Mix all of the ingredients together in a small bowl. Let stand at least 30 minutes at room temperature before serving.

2. To store, place in a tightly sealed container and refrigerate.

NUTRITIONAL FACTS (PER TABLESPOON)
Calories: 8 Carbohydrates: 1.3 g Cholesterol: 0 mg
Fat: 0.2 g Fiber: 0 g Protein: 0.3 g Sodium: 83 mg

Sweet-and-Hot Dipping Sauce

1. Mix all of the ingredients together in a small bowl. Refrigerate at least 30 minutes before using.

2. To store, place in a tightly sealed container and refrigerate.

Yield: 3/4 cup

1/2 cup Rice Dream beverage, or reduced-fat soymilk

2 tablespoons rice vinegar

1 1/2 teaspoons sweet-and-hot mustard sauce

1 clove garlic, minced

NUTRITIONAL FACTS (PER TABLESPOON)
Calories: 12 Carbohydrates: 2.4 g Cholesterol: 0 mg
Fat: 0.2 g Fiber: 0 g Protein: 0 g Sodium: 12 mg

Ginger-and-Vinegar Dipping Sauce

1. Combine all of the ingredients in a small bowl. Refrigerate at least 30 minutes before using.

2. To store, place in a tightly sealed container and refrigerate.

Yield: 3/4 cup

1/4 cup rice vinegar

2 tablespoons lime juice

2 tablespoons minced fresh ginger

1/4 teaspoon sesame oil

NUTRITIONAL FACTS (PER TABLESPOON)
Calories: 2 Carbohydrates: 0.3 g Cholesterol: 0 mg
Fat: 0.1 g Fiber: 0 g Protein: 0 g Sodium: 0.5 mg

4. Rice and Noodles on Display

Rice and noodles are true staples of Chinese-style dishes. Whether prepared simply or combined with other ingredients, rice and noodles serve as both side dishes and main-dish entrées. The true beauty of these two foods is that they are easy to prepare and go well with other foods. What's more, they are low in fat and high in carbohydrates, making them quite filling.

Although some of the ingredients called for in the following recipes may be considered high-fat items—sesame oil, nuts, and beef strips, for instance—realize that they are used quite sparingly. They have been included only for the sake of adding a hint of flavor or color to the dish. And even with these items, the dishes still fall into the very low-fat category.

Rice

In China, rice is as much a part of a meal as bread and potatoes are in the West. Long-grain, short-grain, and sweet rice are the main white rice varieties used in Chinese cooking.

Long-grain rice is narrow in shape and absorbs a lot of water; it is ideal for fried rice

dishes. Short-grain rice is wider than long grain, absorbs less water, and takes longer to cook. This rice is usually served plain as an accompaniment to meals. Both short- and long-grain varieties are found in most grocery stores.

Also known as glutinous rice, sweet rice requires less water than the others and becomes quite sticky when cooked. Many specialty dishes, such as Chicken Rice Rolls (page 66) and Spicy Turkey Rice Rolls (page 63) call for sweet rice. All Asian markets and many health food stores carry sweet rice.

COOKING RICE

I believe the best and simplest way to cook rice is with a rice cooker. Cookers range in price from under twenty dollars for a basic model to well over a hundred dollars for a deluxe model. Although many expensive models offer built-in timers and other special features, know that a basic inexpensive cooker is sufficient. You can probably get the best deal at a store that caters to a large Asian clientele.

All rice cookers come with a specific set of instructions. Basically, all you have to do is place the rinsed rice in the cooking pot, add the specified amount of water, cover the cooker, and push the start button. That's all there is to it. While the rice cooks, you are free to do other things. When the rice is done, if you find it too chewy, mix in a little more water and restart the cooker. If it's too soft or mushy, let the rice cook a little longer (and remember to use less water next time).

If you don't have a cooker, you can use a standard pot to cook rice almost as easily. (Avoid using shallow pans.) As a rule of thumb, when cooking rice, use the following guide:

Types of Rice	Amount (uncooked)	Water	Yield
Long grain	1 cup	2 cups	3 cups
Short grain	1 cup	$1^1/2$ cups	$2^1/2$ cups
Sweet rice (glutinous)	1 cup	$1^1/4$ cups	2 cups

Bring the rice and water to a boil over medium-high heat and cook it for 2 to 3 minutes. Reduce the heat to low and simmer the rice, partially covered, until it is soft and tender (20 to 25 minutes).

The following low-fat rice dishes are tasty, filling, and quick and easy to prepare. Use them as a springboard for creating your own healthful rice variations.

Noodles

The Chinese have always considered the noodle a symbol of longevity. Traditionally, noodles are served at birthday parties as a way of wishing the celebrant a long life.

Whole wheat and rice noodles are the most common varieties used in Chinese cooking. Both are sold in fresh and dry forms. The recipes in this book call for dry noodles, but you can always substitute fresh for dry. However, when using fresh noodles, replace the required amount of dried noodles with $1^1/4$ times as much

fresh. For example, if a recipe calls for 8 ounces of dry noodles, use 10 ounces of fresh. Fresh noodles also cook faster than the dry ones, so be sure to check them as they cook. And always store fresh noodles in the refrigerator.

Translucent rice noodles, which are made from rice flour, come in a variety of widths and thicknesses. Similar in appearance to linguini, rice noodles are often used in soups and cold noodle dishes. The dry variety must be soaked in warm water for five to seven minutes to soften before they can be used. Dry wheat noodles, on the other hand, need no soaking prior to cooking.

Chinese noodles usually come in three approximate widths: $1/16$ inch, $1/8$ inch, and $1/4$ inch. You can easily substitute Italian-style pasta noodles for the Chinese ones. I suggest using fettuccine for the wide noodles, linguini or spaghetti for the thin noodles, and vermicelli or angel hair pasta for the thinnest Chinese noodles.

COOKING NOODLES

Nothing is easier than cooking noodles. Simply bring a pot of water to a boil and add the fresh or dry noodles. As the noodles cook, stir and separate them with a fork. Depending on the thickness of the noodle, cooking times will vary; however, most packages come with instructions. I always test the noodles as they cook to prevent them from overcooking. Noodles should be just barely tender. Unless you are cooking a noodle soup, always drain the cooked noodles in a colander and rinse them with cold water. Cold water helps stop the cooking process, while rinsing away any starch.

A noodle dish is a casual affair that greets any number of ingredients with good cheer. Feel free to exercise your culinary creativity with the following noodle recipes. Add or substitute ingredients for the ones presented. And don't forget to utilize any leftovers or other odds and ends you may have sitting around taking up space in your refrigerator—they can be great additions to noodle dishes. Most of all, have fun with the art of creative cooking.

Top Right: Vegetable Rice with Walnuts (page 62)

Center: Cucumber and Almond Salad with Spicy Dressing (page 93)

Bottom Right: Bai Zai Chicken (page 103)

Top Right: Noodles in Peanut Sauce (page 74)

Center: Spicy Eggplant (page 96)

Bottom Right: Scallops with Orange Peel
(page 123)

Rice

Simple Rice

1. Lightly coat a nonstick wok or frying pan with cooking spray and place over medium heat. Add the cabbage and sauté until the leaves are slightly wilted (about 3 minutes).

2. Add the rice and broth, bring to a boil, then reduce the heat to medium-low. Cover and simmer until the broth is absorbed (3 to 5 minutes).

3. Drizzle the sesame oil over the rice, garnish with green onions, and serve.

Yield: *4 servings*

3 cups cooked short-grain rice

1 cup thinly sliced Napa cabbage

1 cup low-sodium fat-free chicken broth

1/2 teaspoon sesame oil

2 green onions, minced

NUTRITIONAL FACTS (PER 1-CUP SERVING)
Calories: 220 Carbohydrates: 45.7 g Cholesterol: 0 mg
Fat: 0.9 g Fiber: 0.6 g Protein: 4.6 g Sodium: 19 mg

Curried Rice with Green Peas

Simple to prepare, this dish is a great potluck dinner contribution.

1. Mix together the rice, water, curry powder, and pepper in a large pot. Bring to a boil, then reduce the heat to low.

2. Simmer the rice, partially covered, until it is nearly tender (about 20 minutes).

3. Add the peas to the rice, and continue to cook another 5 to 6 minutes.

4. Garnish with green onion and cilantro and serve.

Yield: *4 servings*

2 cups uncooked long-grain rice, rinsed and drained

4 cups water

1 teaspoon curry powder

1 teaspoon ground white pepper

1/2 cup fresh or frozen peas

2 green onions, chopped

1 sprig fresh cilantro, chopped

NUTRITIONAL FACTS (PER 1-CUP SERVING)
Calories: 358 Carbohydrates: 78 g Cholesterol: 0 mg
Fat: 0.7 g Fiber: 2.6 g Protein: 7.9 g Sodium: 19 mg

Vegetable Rice with Walnuts

Yield: 4 servings

3 cups cooked short-grain rice

1 tablespoon minced fresh garlic

1/2 teaspoon Eden Foods sesame shake

1/2 cup fresh or frozen mixed vegetables

1/2 cup chopped green onions

1 tablespoon crushed roasted walnuts (see Roasting Nuts below)

SAUCE

1/4 cup rice vinegar

1 tablespoon sweet-and-hot mustard sauce

1 teaspoon low-sodium soy sauce

Rice readily absorbs the flavors of other ingredients. Feel free to add or substitute other vegetables in this recipe. If your children are obstinate about eating vegetables, perhaps this dish will help change their attitude.

1. Combine the sauce ingredients together in a small bowl and set aside.

2. Lightly coat a nonstick wok or frying pan with cooking spray and place over medium heat. Add the garlic and sesame shake, and sauté until the garlic begins to brown.

3. Add the mixed vegetables and cook until tender.

4. Add the sauce and rice. Mix the ingredients together.

5. Garnish with green onion and walnuts before serving.

NUTRITIONAL FACTS (PER 1-CUP SERVING)

Calories: 234 Carbohydrates: 49 g Cholesterol: 0 mg
Fat: 1.5 g Fiber: 1.2 g Protein: 5 g Sodium: 42 mg

Roasting Nuts

Nuts, which are a natural source of linoleic acid—a polyunsaturated fat that is essential for life—are also a nutritious source of protein. I find myself using nuts, especially walnuts and pecans, more and more as a substitute for meat in a number of dishes. I like to keep roasted varieties on hand to add to a dish at a moment's notice. When properly stored, roasted nuts can stay fresh for a long period of time.

1 pound shelled nuts

1. Place the nuts in a pot with enough cold water to cover and bring to a boil. Drain the nuts and place them on paper towels to air-dry for about an hour.

2. Preheat the oven to 250° F. Spread the nuts in a single layer on a nonstick baking sheet.

3. Roast the nuts, while stirring occasionally, until they are crisp and brown (about 25 to 30 minutes).

4. Allow the nuts to cool before putting them in an air-tight container. Store in the refrigerator or freezer.

Spicy Turkey Rice Rolls

1. Lightly coat a nonstick wok or frying pan with cooking spray and place over medium heat. Add the onion and sauté until soft.

2. Transfer the onion to a large bowl along with the rice, turkey, garlic, and lemon juice. Mix together well and set aside.

3. Bring a pot of water to boil. Add the cabbage leaves and cook until soft (1 to 2 minutes). Remove the leaves and drain.

4. Place about 3 tablespoons of filling in the center of a cabbage leaf. Fold the bottom of the leaf over the filling, followed by the right and left sides. Roll up the leaf and place it cut-side down on a plate. Repeat with the remaining filling and leaves.

5. Steam the rolls 10 to 15 minutes.

6. While the rolls are steaming, bring the sauce ingredients to a boil in a small pot. Remove from the heat.

7. Place the cooked rolls on a platter, top with the sauce, and serve hot.

Yield: 14 rolls

3 cups cooked sweet rice (warm)

8 ounces lean ground turkey

1/2 cup minced white onion

4 cloves garlic, crushed

1 tablespoon fresh lemon juice

14 green cabbage leaves

SAUCE

1/2 cup skim milk or Rice Dream beverage

2 tablespoons mustard sauce

1/4 teaspoon chili pepper flakes

NUTRITIONAL FACTS (PER ROLL)
Calories: 81 Carbohydrates: 14 g Cholesterol: 8 mg
Fat: 0.4 g Fiber: 1 g Protein: 5.3 g Sodium: 41 mg

Red Bean Sweet Rice

***Yield:** 4 servings*

1½ cups uncooked sweet rice, washed and drained

2 cups water

1 cup cooked red beans

¼ cup cooking wine

1 teaspoon ground white pepper

1 sprig fresh cilantro, minced

I find that using a rice cooker is the best method for preparing this dish.

1. Place the rice, water, beans, wine, and pepper in a rice cooker. Cover and cook until the rice is soft (about 20 minutes).

2. Garnish with cilantro and serve.

NUTRITIONAL FACTS (PER 1-CUP SERVING)
Calories: 151 Carbohydrates: 30.2 g Cholesterol: 0 mg
Fat: 0.4 g Fiber: 0.1 g Protein: 6 g Sodium: 92 mg

Party Rice

***Yield:** 4 servings*

3 cups cooked sweet rice (warm)

6 shiitake mushroom caps, diced (if using dried variety, *see* hydrating instructions on page 37)

½ cup cooked chicken strips (*see* page 9)

2 teaspoons chopped garlic

1 tablespoons chopped roasted pecans

2 green onions, chopped

SAUCE

⅓ cup low-sodium soy sauce

¼ cup rice vinegar

2 tablespoons water

1 tablespoon fresh lemon juice

This delicious rice dish is an excellent choice for parties and special dinners.

1. Combine the sauce ingredients in a small bowl and set aside.

2. Lightly coat a nonstick wok or frying pan with cooking spray and place over medium heat. Add the garlic and mushrooms, and sauté until the garlic begins to brown.

3. Add the rice, chicken strips, and sauce. Mix thoroughly.

4. Garnish with pecans and green onion before serving.

NUTRITIONAL FACTS (PER 1-CUP SERVING)
Calories: 244 Carbohydrates: 45.4 g Cholesterol: 12 mg
Fat: 2.8 g Fiber: 2.9 g Protein: 9.4 g Sodium: 294 mg

Rice Stew with Shrimp and Vegetables

This simple dish is ideal to serve on brisk fall or chilly winter evenings.

1. Bring the rice and water to a boil in a large pot. Add the carrots and mushrooms, and reduce the heat to low.

2. Simmer partially covered, and stir occasionally until the rice is soft and tender (about 35 minutes).

3. Add the shrimp, cilantro, green onion, and sesame shake, and cook another 3 minutes.

4. Add the sesame oil and walnuts just before serving.

NUTRITIONAL FACTS (PER 1-CUP SERVING)
Calories: 228 Carbohydrates: 42.1 g Cholesterol: 31 mg
Fat: 2.6 g Fiber: 2.2 g Protein: 7 g Sodium: 103 mg

***Yield:** 4 servings*

1 cup uncooked long-grain rice, rinsed and drained

6 cups water

½ cup grated carrot

4 shiitake mushroom caps, diced (if using dried variety, *see* hydrating instructions on page 37)

½ cup cooked small salad shrimp

2 springs cilantro, chopped

1 green onion, chopped

2 teaspoons Eden Foods sesame shake, or chopped sesame seeds

½ teaspoon sesame oil

2 teaspoons crushed walnuts

Chicken Rice Rolls

Yield: 12 rolls

3 cups cooked sweet rice (warm)

3-ounce skinless chicken breast, finely diced

6 shiitake mushroom caps, minced (if using dried variety, *see* hydrating instructions on page 37)

1/2 cup finely chopped carrot

2 teaspoons minced fresh garlic

1 teaspoon minced fresh ginger

2 green onions, minced

3 sprigs fresh cilantro, minced

1 tablespoon low-sodium soy sauce

2 teaspoons cornstarch

2 tablespoons fresh lemon juice

These rolls can be prepared and stored in the refrigerator, uncooked, for several days. And leftover cooked rolls are great to enjoy the next day.

1. Preheat the oven to 375°F.

2. Lightly coat a nonstick wok or frying pan with cooking spray and place over medium-low heat. Add the chicken and soy sauce, and sauté until the chicken browns (5 to 7 minutes).

3. Transfer the chicken to a large bowl along with all of the remaining ingredients, except the cornstarch and lemon juice.

4. Dissolve the cornstarch in the lemon juice, then add it to the bowl. Mix all the ingredients together well.

5. Scoop a handful of the mixture and form it into a 3-inch-long roll, about $1^1/2$ inches in diameter. Continue making rolls with the remaining mixture.*

6. Wrap each roll individually in aluminum foil, place them on a baking sheet, and bake for 15 minutes.

7. Unwrap the rolls and serve hot or warm.

* Wet your hands with a little cold water before forming the rolls. This will make the sticky mixture easier to work with.

NUTRITIONAL FACTS (PER ROLL)
Calories: 82 Carbohydrates: 15.7 g Cholesterol: 6 mg
Fat: 0.4 g Fiber: 1.1 g Protein: 3.6 g Sodium: 42 mg

Garlic Rice

1. Lightly coat a nonstick wok or frying pan with cooking spray and place it over medium-low heat. Add 2 tablespoons of the garlic and sauté until it starts to brown.

2. Add the rice, broth, and remaining garlic to the pan and mix together well. Cook 2 minutes.

3. Garnish with green onion and serve.

Yield: 4 servings

4 cups cooked long-grain rice

3 tablespoons minced garlic

1/4 cup low-sodium fat-free chicken broth

1 green onion, minced

NUTRITIONAL FACTS (PER 1-CUP SERVING)
Calories: 277 Carbohydrates: 60.9 g Cholesterol: 0 mg
Fat: 0.4 g Fiber: 0.5 g Protein: 5.3 g Sodium: 6 mg

Sweet Rice and Chicken

1. Combine the marinade ingredients in a large bowl. Add the chicken strips, toss to coat, and marinate for 20 minutes.

2. Lightly coat a nonstick wok or frying pan with cooking spray. Place over medium-high heat and stir-fry the chicken. Add the carrots and mushrooms, and cook another 3 minutes.

3. Add the rice and broth and mix well.

4. Garnish with green onion and cilantro before serving.

Yield: 4 servings

3 cups cooked sweet rice (warm)

1/2 cup thinly sliced chicken breast strips

1/2 cup grated carrot

4 shiitake mushroom caps, minced (if using dried variety, *see* hydrating instructions on page 37)

3/4 cup low-sodium fat-free chicken broth

1 green onion, chopped

2 springs fresh cilantro, chopped

MARINADE

1 tablespoon low-sodium soy sauce

1 1/2 teaspoons rice vinegar

1 teaspoon minced fresh ginger

1 teaspoon minced fresh garlic

1/8 teaspoon chili pepper flakes

NUTRITIONAL FACTS (PER 1-CUP SERVING)
Calories: 230 Carbohydrates: 43.3 g Cholesterol: 11 mg
Fat: 1.5 g Fiber: 2.8 g Protein: 8.8 g Sodium: 117 mg

Congee

Yield: *4 servings*

1 cup uncooked long-grain rice, rinsed and drained

6 cups water

2 sprigs cilantro, minced

A rice stew, congee is also known as "rice milk" or "water rice." Depending on the proportion of rice to water, congee can be thick or thin. It is commonly made with other ingredients such as fish, chicken, and lean meats. (see Fish Congee on page 69 and Beef Congee below.)

1. Combine the rice and water in a medium pot, bring to a boil, then reduce the heat to low.

2. Simmer the rice partially covered, and stir occasionally until the rice is soft and tender (about 30 minutes).

3. Sprinkle with cilantro and serve hot or warm.

NUTRITIONAL FACTS (PER 1-CUP SERVING)
Calories: 169 Carbohydrates: 37 g Cholesterol: 0 mg
Fat: 0.3 g Fiber: 0.6 g Protein: 3.3 g Sodium: 2 mg

Beef Congee

Yield: *4 servings*

1 cup uncooked long-grain rice, rinsed and drained

6 cups low-sodium fat-free beef broth

1/2 cup cooked beef strips (*see page 9*)

1 tablespoon minced fresh ginger

2 green onions, minced

The thickness of congee depends on individual preference. If you prefer a thinner congee, simply add more water.

1. Bring the rice and broth to a boil in a large pot. Reduce the heat to low.

2. Simmer partially covered, and stir occasionally until the rice is soft and tender (about 30 minutes).

3. Add the beef and ginger, bring to a boil, and cook for 1 minute.

4. Garnish with green onion and serve.

NUTRITIONAL FACTS (PER 1-CUP SERVING)
Calories: 231 Carbohydrates: 37.9 g Cholesterol: 13 mg
Fat: 0.8 g Fiber: 0.9 g Protein: 15.7 g Sodium: 255 mg

Fish Congee

You can easily replace the fish in this recipe with any type of fish you prefer.

1. Combine the marinade ingredients in a medium bowl. Add the fish, toss to coat, and refrigerate for 20 minutes.

2. Combine the rice, water, and broth in a large pot, bring to a boil, then reduce the heat to low. Simmer partially covered, and stir occasionally until the rice is soft and tender (about 30 minutes).

3. Add the fish, bring to a boil, and cook for 2 minutes.

4. Garnish with green onion and cilantro. Serve hot.

NUTRITIONAL FACTS (PER 1-CUP SERVING)

Calories: 286 Carbohydrates: 50.6 g Cholesterol: 17 mg
Fat: 0.8 g Fiber: 1 g Protein: 12.4 g Sodium: 89 mg

Yield: *6 servings*

2 cups uncooked long-grain rice, rinsed and drained

6 cups cold water

2 cups low-sodium fat-free chicken broth

8 ounces flounder fillet, cut into 2-inch pieces

1 green onion, chopped

1 sprig fresh cilantro, chopped

MARINADE

1 tablespoon rice wine

1 tablespoon low-sodium soy sauce

1 tablespoon fresh lemon juice

1 1/2 teaspoons rice vinegar

2 tablespoons minced fresh ginger

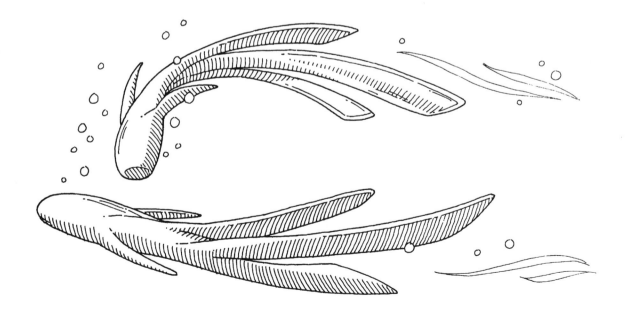

Noodles
Colorful Cold Noodles

You will appreciate this colorful dish during the hot days of summer. It doesn't require much preparation time and its delicious coolness will excite the palate.

1. Mix all of the sauce ingredients together in a small bowl and set aside.

2. Bring a medium-sized pot of water to boil. Add the cucumber, bell pepper, bean sprouts, and peas and cook until soft (1 to 2 minutes). Drain and set aside.

3. Lightly coat an 8-inch nonstick frying pan with cooking spray and place over medium heat. When the pan is hot, pour in the egg substitute and spread it to the edges to make a thin omelet. When the bottom is light brown, flip the omelet and cook the other side. Remove and cut into thin strips.

4. Cook the noodles according to package directions or until just tender. Drain in a colander and rinse with cold water. Drain again, then transfer to a large bowl.

5. Pour the sauce over the noodles and add the eggs, vegetables, and ham. Mix together well.

6. Serve chilled or at room temperature.

NUTRITIONAL FACTS (PER SERVING)
Calories: 154 Carbohydrates: 27.9 g Cholesterol: 2 mg
Fat: 1.8 g Fiber: 1.4 g Protein: 7.3 g Sodium: 282 mg

Yield: 6 servings

8 ounces rice noodles or thin spaghetti

1 small cucumber, cut into thin strips

1 small red bell pepper, thinly sliced

1/2 cup egg substitute

1/4 cup fresh or frozen green peas

1/4 cup bean sprouts

1/4 cup thinly sliced honey-cured ham

SAUCE

3 tablespoons low-sodium soy sauce

2 tablespoons rice vinegar

1 tablespoon commercial or Homemade Chili Paste (page 13)

1 teaspoon white pepper

1/2 teaspoon Eden Foods sesame shake, or chopped sesame seeds

Long Life Noodles in Vegetable Sauce

Yield: *6 servings*

8 ounces wheat noodles or thin spaghetti

2 sprigs fresh cilantro, chopped

SAUCE

1 tablespoon minced fresh garlic

1 medium cucumber, thinly sliced

3 green onions, cut into 2-inch lengths and thinly sliced

½ teaspoon chili pepper flakes

2 cups low-sodium fat-free beef broth

2 tablespoons cornstarch

½ teaspoon ground black pepper

¼ teaspoon five-spice powder

1. Cook the noodles according to package directions or until just tender. Drain in a colander and rinse with cold water. Set aside.

2. Lightly coat a nonstick wok or frying pan with cooking spray and place over medium heat. Add the garlic, cucumber, green onion, and pepper flakes, and sauté until the garlic begins to brown (2 to 3 minutes).

3. Dissolve the cornstarch in the broth and add it to the pan along with the black pepper and five-spice powder. Stir occasionally until the sauce thickens.

4. Add the noodles and toss with the vegetable mixture.

5. Sprinkle with sesame oil, garnish with cilantro, and serve hot.

NUTRITIONAL FACTS (PER SERVING)
Calories: 162 Carbohydrates: 30.8 g Cholesterol: 0 mg
Fat: 1.1 g Fiber: 6 g Protein: 8.3 g Sodium: 63 mg

Noodle Soup

1. Bring the broth to a boil in a medium pot. Add the noodles and bring to a second boil. Reduce the heat, add the peas and seaweed, and continue to cook 2 to 3 minutes.

2. Garnish with the remaining ingredients and serve hot.

Yield: 5 servings

8 ounces wide wheat noodles or fettuccine, cooked

3 cups low-sodium fat-free chicken broth

1/2 cup fresh or frozen green peas

1 tablespoon dry seaweed, or fresh chopped parsley

1/2 green onions, chopped

2 sprigs fresh cilantro, chopped

1 teaspoon sesame oil

NUTRITIONAL FACTS (PER SERVING)

Calories: 198 Carbohydrates: 34.2 g Cholesterol: 0 mg
Fat: 1.7 g Fiber: 7.3 g Protein: 9.4 g Sodium: 60 mg

Noodle Salad

1. Cook the noodles according to package directions or until just tender. Drain in a colander and rinse with cold water. Transfer to a large bowl.

2. Add the bell pepper, carrots, cucumber, and green onion to the noodles and mix well.

3. Mix all of the sauce ingredients together in a small bowl. Pour the sauce over the noodles and toss to coat.

4. Serve cold.

Yield: 6 servings

8 ounces rice noodles or thin spaghetti

1 small red bell pepper, thinly sliced

1 small cucumber, cut into thin strips

1/2 cup grated carrot

2 green onions, cut into 2-inch lengths and thinly sliced

SAUCE

2 tablespoons rice vinegar

2 tablespoons low-sodium teriyaki sauce

2 tablespoons water

1 tablespoon low-sodium soy sauce

1 teaspoon sesame oil

NUTRITIONAL FACTS (PER SERVING)

Calories: 125 Carbohydrates: 25.9 g Cholesterol: 0 mg
Fat: 1.5 g Fiber: 1.1 g Protein: 2.8 g Sodium: 96 mg

Spinach-Topped Noodles

Yield: 7 servings

8 ounces wide wheat noodles or fettuccine

16 ounces fresh spinach, washed thoroughly

3 ounces cooked pork strips (*see page 9*)

1 tablespoon low-sodium soy sauce

1½ teaspoons rice vinegar

2 teaspoons Eden Foods sesame shake, or chopped sesame seeds

½ teaspoon sesame oil

1. Cook the noodles according to package directions or until just tender. Drain in a colander and rinse with cold water. Set aside.

2. Lightly coat a nonstick wok or frying pan with cooking spray and place over medium heat. Add the spinach, and sauté until soft and wilted (3 to 4 minutes).

3. Add the pork, soy sauce, vinegar, and sesame shake. Mix together well and continue to cook another 2 to 3 minutes.

4. Add the noodles and toss with the spinach mixture.

5. Sprinkle with sesame oil and serve immediately.

NUTRITIONAL FACTS (PER SERVING)

Calories: 118 Carbohydrates: 18.5 g Cholesterol: 6 mg
Fat: 2 g Fiber: 5 g Protein: 7 g Sodium: 75 mg

Noodles in Peanut Sauce

Yield: 6 servings

8 ounces wheat noodles or thin spaghetti

SAUCE

½ cup Rice Dream beverage, or reduced-fat soymilk

1½ tablespoons Arrowhead Mills easy-spreading peanut butter

2 teaspoons low-sodium soy sauce

2 teaspoons cornstarch

1 teaspoon rice vinegar

1 teaspoon minced fresh ginger

1 teaspoon minced fresh garlic

1. Cook the noodles according to package directions or until just tender. Drain the noodles in a colander and rinse with cold water. Set aside.

2. Place all of the sauce ingredients in a blender and process until smooth.

3. Transfer the cold noodles to a large bowl. Add the sauce, mix thoroughly, and serve.

NUTRITIONAL FACTS (PER SERVING)

Calories: 174 Carbohydrates: 31.1 g Cholesterol: 0 mg
Fat: 2.7 g Fiber: 5.6 g Protein: 7.2 g Sodium: 68 mg

Seafood Chow Mein

Try substituting fresh squid or scallops for the shrimp in this dish.

Yield: *7 servings*

1. Cook the noodles according to package directions or until just tender. Drain in a colander and rinse with cold water. Set aside.

2. Mix all of the sauce ingredients together in a small bowl and set aside.

3. Lightly coat a nonstick wok or frying pan with cooking spray and place over medium heat. Add the garlic and ginger, and sauté until the garlic begins to brown.

4. Add the shrimp, bean sprouts, onions, and sesame shake. Cook until the onions become clear (about 5 minutes).

5. Add the noodles and sauce to the shrimp and vegetables. Mix thoroughly.

6. Serve hot.

8 ounces wheat noodles or thin spaghetti

8 ounces medium shrimp, deveined

1 cup bean sprouts

1/2 cup chopped white onion

3 cloves garlic, minced

1 tablespoon minced fresh ginger

1 teaspoon Eden Foods sesame shake, or chopped sesame seeds

SAUCE

2 tablespoons hot mustard sauce

1 tablespoon rice vinegar

1 tablespoon cooking wine

1 tablespoon low-sodium soy sauce

NUTRITIONAL FACTS (PER SERVING)

Calories: 170 Carbohydrates: 25 g Cholesterol: 49 mg
Fat: 1.5 g Fiber: 5.2 g Protein: 12.5 g Sodium: 157 mg

Chow Mein with Nuts

Yield: 6 servings

8 ounces wheat noodles or thin
spaghetti

1 cup snow peas

2 tablespoons crushed garlic

1 tablespoon chopped, roasted
walnuts or pecans (see Roasting
Nuts on page 62)

SAUCE

1 tablespoon low-sodium soy sauce

1 tablespoon vinegar

1 tablespoon water

1 teaspoon five-spice powder

1/4 teaspoon chili pepper flakes

*For a spicier taste, substitute curry powder for the five-spice
powder.*

1. Cook the noodles according to package directions or until just
tender. Drain in a colander and rinse with cold water. Set aside.

2. Mix all of the sauce ingredients together in a small bowl
and set aside.

3. Lightly coat a nonstick wok or frying pan with cooking
spray and place over medium heat. Add the garlic and sauté
until it begins to brown.

4. Add noodles, snow peas, and sauce, and mix thoroughly.

5. Garnish with nuts and serve hot.

NUTRITIONAL FACTS (PER SERVING)
Calories: 170 Carbohydrates: 30.1 g Cholesterol: 0 mg
Fat: 2.7 g Fiber: 6.9 g Protein: 7.3 g Sodium: 41 mg

Chicken Chow Mein

Yield: 6 servings

8 ounces wheat noodles or thin
spaghetti

1/2 cup cooked chicken strips (see
page 9)

4 cloves garlic, crushed

1/2 cup low-sodium fat-free chicken
broth

3 green onions, minced

1. Cook the noodles according to package directions or until
just tender. Drain in a colander and rinse with cold water. Set
aside.

2. Lightly coat a nonstick wok or frying pan with cooking
spray and place over medium heat. Add the garlic, and sauté
until it begins to brown.

3. Add the noodles, chicken, and broth to the pan. Mix
together thoroughly.

4. Garnish with green onion and serve warm or cold.

NUTRITIONAL FACTS (PER SERVING)
Calories: 136 Carbohydrates: 22.7 g Cholesterol: 8.3 mg
Fat: 1.6 g Fiber: 4.6 g Protein: 8.2 g Sodium: 41 mg

Cold Noodles with Curry Sauce

1. Cook the noodles according to package directions or until just tender. Drain in a colander and rinse with cold water. Transfer to a serving bowl and set aside.

2. Combine all of the sauce ingredients together in a small saucepan and bring to a boil.

3. Pour the sauce over the noodles, add the green pepper and cucumber, and toss together. Cover and refrigerate.

4. Sprinkle with sesame oil before serving.

Yield: *6 servings*

8 ounces rice noodles or thin spaghetti

1 cup thinly sliced green pepper strips

1 cup thinly sliced cucumber strips

1½ teaspoons sesame oil

SAUCE

2 cups low-sodium fat-free vegetable broth

1½ teaspoons curry paste

½ teaspoon chili pepper flakes

NUTRITIONAL FACTS (PER SERVING)

Calories: 71 Carbohydrates: 15.5 g Cholesterol: 0 mg
Fat: 0.9 g Fiber: 0.4 g Protein: 0.3 g Sodium: 10 mg

Noodles with Meat Sauce

This dish makes an ideal light lunch or snack. For zestier flavor, increase the pepper flakes.

1. Cook the noodles according to package directions or until just tender. Drain in a colander and rinse with cold water. Set aside.

2. Lightly coat a nonstick wok or frying pan with cooking spray and place over medium heat. Add the garlic and pepper flakes, and sauté until the garlic begins to brown.

3. Add the pork and stir-fry until it is no longer pink (2 to 3 minutes). Toss in the cucumber, soy sauce, wine, vinegar, and mustard sauce, and mix well.

4. Add the noodles and mix thoroughly with the meat sauce.

5. Garnish with green onion and serve hot.

Yield: *6 servings*

8 ounces wheat noodles or thin spaghetti

3 green onions, minced

SAUCE

4 ounces extra-lean ground pork

1 tablespoon minced fresh garlic

¼ teaspoon chili pepper flakes

½ cup cucumber strips

2 tablespoons low-sodium soy sauce

2 tablespoons cooking wine

1 tablespoon rice vinegar

1 teaspoon mustard sauce

NUTRITIONAL FACTS (PER SERVING)

Calories: 156 Carbohydrates: 23.6 g Cholesterol: 8 mg
Fat: 3.3 g Fiber: 4.8 g Protein: 7.5 g Sodium: 77 mg

5. Tofu Creations

Every country has a food that is part of its national identity—a food that everyone seems to love. Tofu, which has been a mainstay in China and other countries in the Orient for over two thousand years, is one of these foods.

It is believed that tofu (also called bean curd), which is made from soybeans, was created by Chinese Buddhist monks. Brought to Japan by these Buddhist missionaries, tofu was first enjoyed only by members of the upper class. Today, in both China and Japan, tofu is eaten by everyone, rich and poor. Its easy digestibility makes it a perfect food for the elderly as well as for babies.

Although tofu was first brought to the United States in the middle 1800s by Chinese immigrants, it wasn't until the 1970s that it began to gain in popularity. Diet-conscious Americans, both vegetarian and nonvegetarian, began to take notice of this healthy, ecological, and economical food.

Nutritionally, tofu has often been labeled the "perfect" food. Low in sodium and fat, tofu has absolutely no cholesterol. An excellent source of protein, tofu contains all eight of the essential amino acids that the body cannot produce. It is also high in calcium, potassium, important B vitamins (niacin, riboflavin, thiamine), and vitamin E. Although tofu does have some fat, it is primarily the monounsaturated and polyunsaturated types—the "good fats"—that are present. (*See* discussion on Importance of Fighting Fat, beginning on page 3.)

Tofu's nutritional value and digestibility are not the only reasons for its growing popularity. It is also very adaptable to its surrounding ingredients. Basically a fresh but bland-tasting food, tofu's porous texture enables it to readily absorb the flavors of the ingredients with which it is cooked. This makes it deliciously unique and versatile—you can make tofu taste like just about anything.

TOFU TYPES

Generally, tofu is sold in extra-firm, firm, and soft (silken) types. Firm varieties are made by pressing the curds tightly to eliminate as much water as possible. For soft tofu, the curds are not pressed at all but are allowed to set with the whey. The result is a creamy product that is good to use in dips, sauces, and a variety of creamy desserts.

Generally sold in 16-ounce blocks that are

packaged in water, firm tofu can be sliced, diced, or crumbled and used as a meat replacement in stir-fry dishes, soups, and stews. It is also a good substitute for the eggs in scrambled eggs and egg salad. Sautéed with your favorite spices, tofu is delicious served over rice or noodles.

Several companies package tofu in aseptic paper containers that need no refrigeration. This packaging extends the tofu's shelf life and is a convenient way of always having tofu on hand. I have found, however, that tofu packaged this way does not freeze as well as the water-packed variety.

Recently, fresh tofu with a very low fat content has appeared on store shelves. One company, Mori-Nu, packages 10.5-ounce blocks of firm and extra-firm tofu that have only 1 gram of fat per 3-ounce serving (most regular tofu varieties contain in excess of 6 grams of fat for the same amount.) Although Mori Nu is my tofu brand of choice—and the one used for the nutritional analysis in this book—there are other reduced-fat brands I use when the dish requires a very firm tofu (even the firm Mori Nu tofu is a bit softer than other firm varieties). White Wave brand, for instance, offers firm, reduced-fat tofu with 4 grams of fat per 3.2-ounce serving.

Many health food stores and Oriental markets carry baked tofu, which is drier and darker in color than fresh tofu. Also called dry tofu or *doufugan,* this tofu is not actually "dry." It is fresh tofu that has been pressed until it is very dense, resulting in a very firm-textured product—ideal as a meat substitute. Many commercial brands of baked tofu are flavored and tend to be high in both fat and sodium. For this reason, I suggest making your own baked tofu (*see* instructions in the following section).

MAKING BAKED TOFU

Not only is making your own baked tofu easy, it results in a product that is lower in fat and sodium than most commercial brands.

To make 12 ounces of baked tofu, start with a 16-ounce block of fresh low-fat tofu. Slice the block lengthwise into three equal pieces, then quarter each piece. Arrange the pieces on a baking sheet that has been lightly coated with cooking spray, and place in a preheated 450°F oven. Bake about 15 minutes, or until the tops are light brown, then turn the pieces over and brown the other side. Allow the tofu to cool before using. To store, wrap the pieces in plastic wrap and place them in the refrigerator.

STORING TOFU

Fresh firm tofu is generally packaged in water-filled containers and found in the produce section of most grocery stores. Perishable, tofu should be kept refrigerated. Some stores sell loose, unpacked blocks of tofu that are immersed in water. To help ensure freshness, keep it refrigerated and change the water daily. Tofu that comes in aseptic containers needs no refrigeration but must be used before the expiration date.

Fresh tofu has a slightly sweet smell. If it starts to smell a little sour, boil it for ten minutes or so to restore its freshness. When boiled, the tofu will become a little spongy.

Tofu also freezes well. Simply drain the fresh tofu and squeeze out the excess water. Place the tofu in a freezer bag or a tightly sealed container and store it in the freezer where it will keep for up to five months. As the tofu freezes, its color will change from white to tan. Defrost the tofu at room temperature; if you are in a hurry, you can immerse it in warm water. Before preparing the defrosted tofu, rinse it and press out the excess water. It will have a firmer, spongier, chewier texture—similar to tender meat—than it had before it was frozen.

The following recipes highlight tofu's goodness in nutritious low-fat dishes. I hope you will find them delicious as well.

Cabbage Rolls

1. In a medium bowl, mash the tofu with a spoon. Add all of the remaining filling ingredients, except the cornstarch. Dissolve the cornstarch in a tablespoon of water and add it to the bowl. Mix the ingredients together well.

2. Cut the cabbage leaves into 4-x-6-inch squares. Blanch in boiling water until soft. Pat dry.

3. Place the leaves on a flat surface. Spoon 2 rounded tablespoons of filling in the center of each leaf. Fold the left and right sides over the filling, then, starting at the bottom, roll the leaves up to form neatly filled packets.

4. Place the rolls on a steamer rack set over boiling water. Cover and steam the rolls for 15 to 20 minutes.

5. When the cabbage rolls are almost cooked, bring the sauce ingredients to a boil in a small pan.

6. Place the cooked rolls on a serving platter, spoon the sauce on top, and serve hot.

NUTRITIONAL FACTS (PER ROLL)
Calories: 35 Carbohydrates: 2.2 g Cholesterol: 7 mg
Fat: 0.8 g Fiber: 0.4 g Protein: 4.9 g Sodium: 36 mg

Yield: *12 rolls*

12 cabbage leaves (Napa, Peking, or green)

FILLING

8 ounces soft low-fat tofu

6 ounces extra-lean ground turkey or chicken

4 shiitake mushroom caps, diced (if using dried variety, *see* hydrating instructions on page 37)

¼ cup diced carrots

1 egg white

1 tablespoon rice vinegar

1½ teaspoons low-sodium soy sauce

½ teaspoon five-spice powder

½ teaspoon cornstarch

SAUCE

¼ cup low-sodium fat-free chicken broth

½ teaspoon cornstarch

1 teaspoon honey mustard

Crabmeat Tofu

Yield: *5 servings*

16 ounces firm low-fat tofu, cut into 1/2-inch cubes

1 teaspoon chopped ginger

3 ounces fresh crabmeat, finely flaked*

1/2 cup fresh or frozen corn kernels

2 teaspoons cornstarch

1/2 cup water

1 teaspoon Mrs. Dash seasoning

1/2 teaspoon five-spice powder

1/2 teaspoon ground black pepper

1 green onion, chopped

* Can use artificial variety.

1. Lightly coat a nonstick wok or frying pan with cooking spray and place over medium heat. Add the ginger and sauté for a minute, then add the tofu, crabmeat, and corn. Stir-fry for 2 to 3 minutes.

2. Dissolve the cornstarch in the water and add it to the pan along with the remaining ingredients.

3. Continue to stir-fry the ingredients until the tofu and crabmeat are coated with a light, clear glaze (2 to 3 minutes).

4. Garnish with green onion and serve hot.

NUTRITIONAL FACTS (PER SERVING)

Calories: 76 Carbohydrates: 4.8 g Cholesterol: 13 mg
Fat: 1.5 g Fiber: 0.6 g Protein: 10 g Sodium: 144 mg

Tofu Oriental

Yield: *5 servings*

16 ounces firm low-fat tofu

1 teaspoon Arrowhead Mills easy-spreading peanut butter

1 teaspoon low-sodium soy sauce

1/4 teaspoon sesame oil

4 green onions, chopped

4 cloves garlic, minced

Serve this refreshing dish on a hot summer day.

1. Bring a medium pot of water to a boil and add the tofu. Allow the water to come to a second boil, then remove the tofu and drain.

2. Place the tofu on a clean cutting board and cut it into 1/2-inch cubes.

3. Combine the peanut butter, soy sauce, and sesame oil in a bowl. Add the tofu cubes and gently toss to coat. Sprinkle with green onion and garlic, cover, and refrigerate at least 30 minutes.

4. Serve chilled.

NUTRITIONAL FACTS (PER SERVING)

Calories: 66 Carbohydrates: 3.2 g Cholesterol: 0 mg
Fat: 2.5 g Fiber: 0.6 g Protein: 7.6 g Sodium: 125 mg

Tofu-Pineapple Kebobs

To prevent the tofu cubes from falling apart as they cook, be sure to use a very firm type of tofu.

1. Cut the block of tofu into 24 cubes (*see* figure below).

2. Combine the marinade ingredients in a bowl. Add the tofu cubes and toss to coat. Marinate at room temperature for 1 hour.

3. Thread six skewers with alternating pieces of pineapple, marinated tofu, bell pepper, and onion. (Each kebob should have 2 tofu cubes, 3 pineapple cubes, 2 bell pepper squares, and 1 onion wedge.)

4. Brush the kebobs with marinade before placing them on a hot grill.

5. Grill the kebobs, occasionally turning and basting them with marinade, until the edges of the peppers are brown and crisp (10 to 15 minutes).

6. Serve hot with rice or noodles.

Yield: *12 kebobs*

16-ounce block extra-firm low-fat tofu

36 pineapple cubes (1 inch)

1 large red bell pepper, cut into 12 squares (1 inch)

1 large yellow or green bell pepper, cut into 12 squares (1 inch)

1 red onion, cut into 12 wedges

MARINADE

1/4 cup water

4 cloves garlic, minced

2 tablespoons low-sodium teriyaki sauce

2 teaspoons minced fresh ginger

1 1/2 teaspoons honey mustard

NUTRITIONAL FACTS (PER KEBOB)

Calories: 43 Carbohydrates: 6.2 g Cholesterol: 0 mg
Fat: 0.6 g Fiber: 0.7 g Protein: 3 g Sodium: 76 mg

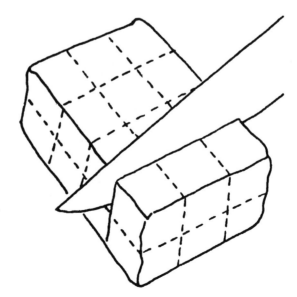

Slice the tofu lengthwise and crosswise to form cubes.

Spicy Tofu with Green Peas

Yield: 5 servings

For added flavor include extra-lean ground beef or chicken.

16 ounces extra-firm low-fat tofu, cut into 1/2-inch cubes

1/4 cup fresh or frozen green peas

4 cloves garlic, minced

1 green onion, chopped

SAUCE

1/2 cup cold water

2 tablespoons cornstarch

1 teaspoon commercial or Home-made Chili Paste (page 13)

1 teaspoon Mrs. Dash seasoning

1. To make the sauce, combine the cornstarch and water in a small bowl. Add the remaining sauce ingredients and mix well. Set aside.

2. Lightly coat a nonstick wok or frying pan with cooking spray and place over medium heat. Add the garlic and sauté until it begins to brown.

3. Add the tofu and cook for 1 to 2 minutes. Raise the heat to medium-high, add the green peas and sauce, and bring to a boil. Cook another 2 minutes or until the sauce thickens.

4. Garnish with green onion and serve.

NUTRITIONAL FACTS (PER SERVING)

Calories: 61 Carbohydrates: 5.3 g Cholesterol: 0 mg
Fat: 1 g Fiber: 0.5 g Protein: 7 g Sodium: 121 mg

Sweet-and-Sour Tofu

Yield: 5 servings

To prepare your own dry tofu, see Making Baked Tofu on page 80.

16 ounces dry tofu, cut into 1/2-inch cubes

4 cloves garlic, crushed

1 small green bell pepper, seeded and cut into squares

1 small red bell pepper, seeded and cut into squares

1 cup Rice Dream beverage, or reduced-fat soymilk

1 teaspoon cornstarch

2 tablespoons sweet-and-sour sauce

1/2 teaspoon five-spice powder

1. Lightly coat a nonstick wok or frying pan with cooking spray and place over medium heat. Add the tofu and cook until brown. Transfer to a serving bowl.

2. Recoat the pan with cooking spray. Add the garlic, and sauté until it begins to brown. Add the bell peppers and stir-fry briefly.

3. Dissolve the cornstarch in the Rice Dream and add it to the pan along with the sweet-and-sour sauce and five-spice powder. Stir the ingredients together and bring to a boil.

4. Spoon the peppers over the tofu and serve.

NUTRITIONAL FACTS (PER SERVING)

Calories: 94 Carbohydrates: 11.6 g Cholesterol: 0 mg
Fat: 2.2 g Fiber: 0.6 g Protein: 8.2 g Sodium: 133 mg

Top Left: *Colorful Spicy Vegetable Soup (page 24)*
Center: *Sautéed Shrimp with Snow Peas (page 121)*
Bottom Left: *Noodle Salad (page 73)*

Top Right: Asparagus in Orange-Ginger Sauce (page 98)

Bottom: Shredded Szechuan Pork (page 102)

East Meets West Tofu

1. Place the tofu on a heatproof plate, then set it on a steamer rack over boiling water. Steam the tofu for 5 to 7 minutes, then transfer it to a serving dish.

2. Lightly coat a nonstick wok or frying pan with cooking spray and place it over medium heat. Add the bell peppers, ginger, and garlic, and sauté until the peppers begin to soften (2 to 3 minutes). Transfer to a bowl.

3. Place all of the sauce ingredients, except the cornstarch, in the pan over medium heat. Stir together well. Dissolve the cornstarch in 2 tablespoons of water, add it to the pan and bring the sauce to a boil.

4. Return the sautéed peppers to the pan and combine with the sauce.

5. Spoon the peppers over the tofu. Slice and serve.

NUTRITIONAL FACTS (PER SERVING)
Calories: 70 Carbohydrates: 5.1 g Cholesterol: 0 mg
Fat: 1.1 g Fiber: 0.3 g Protein: 6.8 g Sodium: 86 mg

Yield: 5 servings

16-ounce block firm low-fat tofu

1/3 cup thinly sliced green bell pepper

1/3 cup thinly sliced red bell pepper

3 tablespoons grated ginger

4 cloves garlic, minced

SAUCE

1/4 cup water

2 tablespoons white vinegar

1 tablespoon sugar

1 1/2 teaspoons low-sodium ketchup

1 teaspoon cornstarch

Three Threads Tofu

Yield: 4 servings

8 ounces extra-firm low-fat tofu, chilled and sliced into thin strips

1½ cups thinly sliced red bell pepper

1½ cups thinly sliced green bell pepper

SAUCE

½ cup water

2 teaspoons Eden Foods sesame shake, or chopped sesame seeds

1 tablespoon extra-hot mustard

½ teaspoon five-spice powder

The thin strips of tofu and the red and green peppers make up the "threads" of this all-season dish. Be sure to gently press the water from the tofu before slicing it.

1. Lightly coat a nonstick wok or frying pan with cooking spray and place over medium heat.

2. Add the tofu and gently stir-fry until it is brown (2 to 3 minutes). Transfer the tofu to a serving dish.

3. Recoat the pan with cooking spray and stir-fry the peppers until they just begin to soften (about 1 minute). Arrange the peppers on top of the tofu.

4. Bring the sauce ingredients to a boil in a small saucepan. Pour the sauce over the tofu and peppers. Serve immediately.

NUTRITIONAL FACTS (PER SERVING)

Calories: 40 Carbohydrates: 4.1 g Cholesterol: 0 mg
Fat: 1 g Fiber: 0.4 g Protein: 4.2 g Sodium: 84 mg

Chinese Lantern Festival

The fifteen-day long Chinese New Year's celebration ends with the Lantern Festival on the night of the year's first full moon. Unlike the New Year's celebration, in which the focus is on the family, the Lantern Festival involves the entire community. On the day of the festival, friends and relatives spend time visiting each other. Traditionally, matchmakers spend the day traveling between the homes of eligible young people in an attempt to arrange marriages.

At night, community members gather together to display their lanterns, which are usually made of silk or paper and come in a variety of shapes. The Chinese believe that evil spirits roam freely on the night of the first full moon of the new year. They also believe that the soft light of the lanterns will ward off these evil spirits, who avoid the light because it makes them visible.

During the Lantern Festival, everyone eats Tang Yuan or full moon dumplings. These sweet-tasting rice-flour balls are stuffed with a variety of fillings, then boiled and served in a light soup (for recipe, see page 133). The round, white Tang Yuan are symbolic of the full moon and the family union. The Chinese believe that by eating these sweet rice balls in the light of the bright lanterns, they will become focused and clear-sighted.

For information on the Chinese New Year's celebration, which precedes the Lantern Festival, see page 43.

Tofu-Stuffed Green Peppers

1. To make the stuffing, mash the tofu in a large bowl, then add the mushrooms, shrimp, garlic, Mrs. Dash seasoning, and sesame oil. Dissolve the cornstarch in the water and add it to the bowl. Mix the ingredients together well.

2. Fill the green pepper halves with the stuffing, and place them on a steamer rack that is set over boiling water. Cover and steam for 10 to 12 minutes.

3. When the peppers are nearly cooked, bring the sauce ingredients to a boil in a small pan.

4. Place the cooked stuffed peppers on a serving platter, top with the sauce, and serve.

NUTRITIONAL FACTS (PER STUFFED PEPPER)

Calories: 65 Carbohydrates: 4.8 g Cholesterol: 24 mg
Fat: 1.4 g Fiber: 0.9 g Protein: 8.2 g Sodium: 146 mg

Yield: 6 servings

3 medium-large green bell peppers, halved and seeded

STUFFING

16 ounces firm low-fat tofu

2 shiitake mushroom caps, diced (if using dried variety, *see* hydrating instructions on page 37)

3 tablespoons cooked small salad shrimp

4 cloves garlic, minced

1 teaspoon Mrs. Dash seasoning

1/2 teaspoon sesame oil

1 teaspoon cornstarch

2 teaspoons water

SAUCE

1/4 cup low-sodium fat-free chicken broth

1 teaspoon low-sodium teriyaki sauce

1/2 teaspoon cornstarch

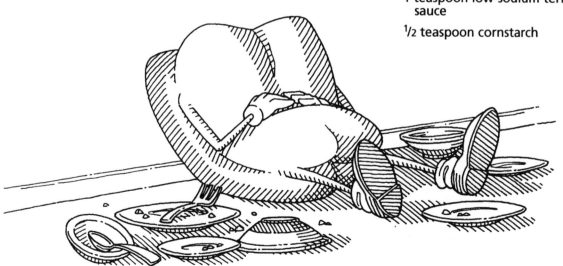

Four Seasons Tofu

Yield: 8 servings

16 ounces soft low-fat tofu

4 ounces medium shrimp, deveined

2 tablespoons minced fresh ginger

2 teaspoons sesame oil

5 shiitake mushroom caps, diced (if using dry variety, *see* hydrating instructions on page 37)

1/4 cup diced carrots

1/4 cup fresh or frozen corn kernels

2 teaspoons five-spice powder

1 teaspoon Mrs. Dash seasoning

1/2 cup egg substitute

3 green onions, minced

3 sprigs fresh cilantro, minced

1. Preheat the oven to 350°F. Lightly coat a 9-x-9-inch baking dish with cooking spray and set aside.

2. Place the tofu, shrimp, ginger, and sesame oil in a blender or food processor and blend into a "jelly." Transfer to a medium bowl.

3. Lightly coat a nonstick wok or frying pan with cooking spray and place over medium heat. Add the mushrooms, carrots, and corn, and sauté about 3 minutes. Stir in the five-spice powder and Mrs. Dash seasoning. Combine with the tofu mixture.

4. Spread the mixture evenly in the baking dish and place in the oven.

5. Bake for 20 minutes, then remove from the oven and brush the egg subsitute in a thin layer on top. Return to the oven and bake until golden brown (about 5 minutes).

6. Garnish with green onion and cilantro. Serve hot.

NUTRITIONAL FACTS (PER SERVING)

Calories: 79 Carbohydrates: 6.4 g Cholesterol: 22 mg
Fat: 2.7 g Fiber: 0.8 g Protein: 6.4 g Sodium: 53 mg

Szechuan Cooking

Located in the western region, Szechuan is China's largest and most populated province. Its climate is hot and almost tropical, and its food is similar. Characteristically peppery hot and spicy, Szechuan (sometimes called Chunking) dishes have become increasingly popular in the United States in recent years. Hot and sour soup and highly spiced pork, tofu, and poultry dishes are popular regional offerings. Spicy vegetables, like the Dry-Cooked Green Beans in Szechuan Sauce on page 95, are also standard fare. Although food from this region is often fatty and somewhat oily, I have presented delicious yet low-fat versions. Be sure to try Ma Po's Tofu on page 89 and Shredded Szechuan Pork on page 102 for a taste of this spicy regional cooking.

Ma Po's Tofu

1. Prepare the seasoning blend. In a small bowl, dissolve the cornstarch in the water, then add the remaining seasoning-blend ingredients. Stir to combine and set aside.

2. Lightly coat a nonstick wok or frying pan with cooking spray and place over high heat. Stir-fry the pork and garlic until the meat is cooked (2 to 3 minutes). Add the five-spice powder and cook another 2 minutes.

3. Mix in the chili paste.

4. Add the tofu and seasoning-blend mixture to the wok, and bring the ingredients to a boil. Reduce the heat to medium-low and cook until the juice thickens (1 to 2 minutes)

5. Transfer to a serving bowl, garnish with green onions and sesame oil, and serve.

NUTRITIONAL FACTS (PER SERVING)
Calories: 75 Carbohydrates: 4.4 g Cholesterol: 4 mg
Fat: 2.8 g Fiber: 0.2 g Protein: 7.8 g Sodium: 135 mg

Yield: 5 servings

16 ounces extra-firm low-fat tofu, cut into 1/2-inch cubes

2 ounces extra-lean ground pork

5 cloves garlic, minced

1/4 teaspoon five-spice powder

1 teaspoon commercial or Home-made Chili Paste (page 13)

2 fresh green onions, minced

1/2 teaspoon sesame oil

SEASONING BLEND

1 tablespoon cornstarch

3 tablespoons water

1/4 cup Rice Dream beverage, or reduced-fat soymilk

1 teaspoon low-sodium soy sauce

1 teaspoon rice vinegar

1 tablespoon Mrs. Dash seasoning

6. Vegetarian Pleasers

I have loved vegetables for as long as I can remember. That is until I tried American varieties, which I found to be either overcooked and tasteless or deep-fried and greasy. I can't help but feel sorry for those children who don't want to finish their vegetables at mealtime. I believe if vegetables looked more attractive and tasted better, children would love them just as much as I did when I was young.

Buddhism, the dominant religion of China, has relied on vegetables and tofu as dietary staples for centuries. This demonstrates that a proper vegetarian diet can meet all of a person's nutritional needs. Not surprisingly, some of the best vegetable dishes originated in Buddhist monasteries.

To make scrumptious vegetable dishes, always start with fresh high-quality vegetables. The refrigerator can be invaluable in preserving freshness, moisture, and the vitamin content of most vegetables. Be aware, however, that not all vegetables benefit from refrigeration. Yellow onions and certain types of squash, for example, are best kept in a cool, dark place.

Keep the following helpful tips in mind for the optimal preservation and preparation of vegetables:

- Never wash vegetables until you are ready to use them. Washing causes the vegetables to quickly wilt or rot (even if they are refrigerated).

- Minimize the time that vegetables are kept at room temperature, and make sure they are dry before refrigerating. This will help preserve their freshness and vitamin content.

- Do not peel or cut vegetables until you are ready to cook them.

- Always thaw frozen vegetables and drain them of excess moisture before using.

Through cooking methods such as steaming and stir-frying, most fresh vegetables can retain their flavor, color, and crispness, as well as their valuable nutrients. Cooking times will vary, however, depending on a variety of factors—type and age of the vegetables, size of the pieces, type of pan used, and amount of heat used. The secret to perfectly cooked vegetables is to check them as they cook and remove them from the heat as soon as they are done. It is wiser to keep an eye on the vegetables rather than on the clock.

The following side dishes are, nutritious, delicious, and low in fat. They will please even the most finicky vegetable eaters.

Cucumber and Almond Salad with Spicy Dressing

1. Combine the dressing ingredients in a medium bowl. Add the cucumber slices and toss to coat. Refrigerate for 30 minutes.

2. Garnish with almonds and serve chilled.

NUTRITIONAL FACTS (PER SERVING)

Calories: 47 Carbohydrates: 5.6 g Cholesterol: 0 mg
Fat: 1.6 g Fiber: 1.8 g Protein: 1.5 g Sodium: 54 mg

Yield: *4 servings*

3 cups 1/4-inch-thick cucumber slices

2 teaspoons slivered almonds

DRESSING

1 tablespoon rice vinegar

2 teaspoons minced fresh garlic

2 teaspoons low-sodium soy sauce

2 teaspoons Eden Foods sesame shake, or chopped sesame seeds

1/2 teaspoon sesame oil

1/2 teaspoon chili pepper flakes

1/2 teaspoon sugar

Celery Salad with Shrimp

1. Combine the marinade ingredients in a medium bowl. Add the shrimp, toss to coat, and marinate in the refrigerator for 30 minutes.

2. Bring a medium pot of water to a boil. Add the celery and cook until it just begins to soften (2 to 3 minutes). Drain.

3. Add the celery, sesame shake, and sesame oil to the shrimp. Mix thoroughly and refrigerate another 30 minutes.

4. Serve chilled.

NUTRITIONAL FACTS (PER SERVING)

Calories: 62 Carbohydrates: 3.7 g Cholesterol: 43 mg
Fat: 1.9 g Fiber: 1.8 g Protein: 6.6 g Sodium: 191 mg

Yield: *4 servings*

3 cups sliced celery

1/2 cup cooked small salad shrimp

1/2 teaspoon Eden Foods sesame shake, or chopped sesame seeds

1/2 teaspoon sesame oil

MARINADE

1 tablespoon cooking wine

1 tablespoon white vinegar

1 teaspoon low-sodium soy sauce

Spinach with Sesame Seeds

Yield: *4 servings*

16 ounces fresh spinach, thoroughly washed

1/2 teaspoon sesame oil

1 tablespoon toasted sesame seeds

DRESSING

2 teaspoons cooking wine

2 teaspoons low-sodium soy sauce

1 green onion, minced

1 1/2 teaspoons minced fresh ginger

1/2 teaspoon Eden Foods sesame shake, or chopped sesame seeds

1/4 teaspoon Mrs. Dash extra-spicy seasoning

For a spark of flavor, add some chili pepper flakes or hot chili oil (page 16) to the dressing.

1. Bring 4 cups of water to a boil in a medium pot. Add the spinach and blanch until the leaves are bright green (do not overcook). Drain, rinse with cold water, and drain again. Place in a serving bowl to cool. Add the sesame oil and toss the spinach to coat.

2. Combine the dresssing ingredients in a small bowl. Mix well and add to the spinach.

3. Sprinkle with sesame shake and serve warm or chilled.

NUTRITIONAL FACTS (PER SERVING)

Calories: 48 Carbohydrates: 4.6 g Cholesterol: 0 mg
Fat: 2.1 g Fiber: 3.3 g Protein: 3.9 g Sodium: 158 mg

Tomato Salad

Yield: *4 servings*

1 pound ripe tomatoes, cut into bite-sized cubes

6 cloves garlic, minced

1 tablespoon low-sodium soy sauce

1 teaspoon extra-virgin olive oil

1 1/2 teaspoons rice vinegar

1/2 teaspoon ground black pepper

1 sprig cilantro, chopped

1. Mix all of the ingredients, except the cilantro, together in a bowl. Refrigerate for 15 minutes, stir the ingredients again, and refrigerate another 15 minutes.

2. Garnish with cilantro and serve.

NUTRITIONAL FACTS (PER SERVING)

Calories: 29 Carbohydrates: 5.9 g Cholesterol: 0 mg
Fat: 0.6 g Fiber: 0.8 g Protein: 1.2 g Sodium: 9 mg

Dry-Cooked Green Beans in Szechuan Sauce

1. Mix the sauce ingredients together in a small bowl and set aside.

2. Lightly coat a nonstick wok or frying pan with cooking spray and place over medium-low heat. Add the garlic and sauté until it begins to brown.

3. Increase the heat to medium and add the canola oil and beans. Stir-fry the beans until they become wrinkled (10 to 12 minutes). Add the sesame shake and mix thoroughly.

4. Add the sauce, reduce the heat to medium-low, and stir frequently to prevent burning. Allow the sauce to cook down (about 4 minutes), then remove from the heat.

5. Garnish with green onion and serve.

Yield: 4 servings

3 cups green beans, tips removed*

2 teaspoons minced fresh garlic

1 teaspoon canola oil

1 teaspoon Eden Foods sesame shake, or chopped sesame seeds

2 green onions, minced

SAUCE

¼ cup water

1½ teaspoons low-sodium soy sauce

1½ teaspoons commercial or Homemade Chili Paste (page 13)

½ teaspoon sugar

* If beans are long, break them into 3-inch pieces.

NUTRITIONAL FACTS (PER SERVING)
Calories: 47 Carbohydrates: 7.8 g Cholesterol: 0 mg
Fat: 1.4 g Fiber: 2.3 g Protein: 1.8 g Sodium: 90 mg

Spicy Eggplant

Yield: 4 servings

1 pound eggplant, cut (unpeeled) into 2-inch cubes

1 tablespoon minced fresh garlic

1 teaspoon canola oil

1 green onion, chopped

SAUCE

1 tablespoon low-sodium soy sauce

1 tablespoon water

1 teaspoon rice vinegar

1/2 teaspoon sugar

1/2 teaspoon Mrs. Dash extra-spicy seasoning

1. Combine the sauce ingredients in a small bowl and set aside.

2. Lightly coat a nonstick wok or frying pan with cooking spray, add the oil, and place over medium heat. Add the garlic and sauté until it begins to brown.

3. Increase the heat, add the oil and eggplant, and stir-fry until the eggplant is soft (2 to 3 minutes). Stir the sauce in and remove from the heat.

4. Transfer the eggplant to a serving bowl, garnish with green onion, and serve.

NUTRITIONAL FACTS (PER SERVING)
Calories: 47 Carbohydrates: 8.7 g Cholesterol: 0 mg
Fat: 1.4 g Fiber: 3 g Protein: 1.5 g Sodium: 55 mg

Hot-and-Sour Cabbage

Yield: 4 servings

1 small head Napa cabbage

4 cloves garlic, crushed

1/2 teaspoon Mrs. Dash extra-spicy seasoning

2 green onions, minced

SAUCE

1 tablespoon cornstarch

1/2 cup low-sodium fat-free chicken broth

1/4 cup low-sodium ketchup

1. Cut the cabbage leaves crosswise into 2-inch-wide strips. Set aside.

2. To prepare the sauce, dissolve the cornstarch in the broth, then stir in the ketchup. Set aside.

3. Lightly coat a nonstick wok or frying pan with cooking spray and place over medium heat. Add the garlic and sauté until it begins to brown.

4. Add the cabbage and Mrs. Dash seasoning, and cook for 3 to 4 minutes. Pour the sauce over the cabbage and continue to cook until the cabbage is soft (about 1 minute).

5. Garnish with green onion and serve hot.

NUTRITIONAL FACTS (PER SERVING)
Calories: 39 Carbohydrates: 8.6 g Cholesterol: 0 mg
Fat: 0.2 g Fiber: 0.9 g Protein: 1.2 g Sodium: 16 mg

Cold Eggplant in Garlic Sauce

1. Bring the eggplant and 3 cups of cold water to boil in a medium pot. Cook the eggplant until it is soft (7 to 10 minutes).

2. Drain the eggplant thoroughly, place in a serving bowl, and refrigerate for 20 minutes.

3. Combine the sauce ingredients in a small bowl and mix well. Add to the chilled eggplant, mix thoroughly, and serve.

NUTRITIONAL FACTS (PER SERVING)

Calories: 35 Carbohydrates: 7 g Cholesterol: 0 mg
Fat: 0.4 g Fiber: 2.4 g Protein: 1.1 g Sodium: 294 mg

Yield: 4 Servings

1 pound eggplant, cut (unpeeled) into $\frac{1}{2}$-inch-thick strips

SAUCE

2 tablespoons low-sodium teriyaki sauce

2 tablespoons fat-free Italian salad dressing

3 cloves garlic, minced

1 green onion, chopped

1 teaspoon minced fresh ginger

Asparagus in Orange-Ginger Sauce

Yield: 4 servings

3 cups fresh asparagus spears, diagonally cut into 2-inch lengths

2 tablespoons minced fresh garlic

1/2 teaspoon Eden Foods sesame shake, or chopped sesame seeds

1/2 teaspoon Mrs. Dash seasoning

SAUCE

1/4 cup rice vinegar

2 tablespoons orange juice

1 tablespoon minced orange peel

1 teaspoon minced fresh ginger

This dish is quick and easy to prepare. If you are in a hurry, use frozen asparagus. You can also sauté the asparagus rather than blanch it for a richer flavor.

1. Thoroughly combine the sauce ingredients in a small bowl and set aside.

2. Bring 4 cups of water to a boil in a medium pot. Add the asparagus and blanch until it is soft but not mushy (1 to 2 minutes) Drain and place in a serving bowl.

3. Pour the sauce over the asparagus, add the garlic, and toss to coat.

4. Sprinkle with sesame shake and Mrs. Dash seasoning. Serve hot.

NUTRITIONAL FACTS (PER SERVING)
Calories: 35 Carbohydrates: 6.7 g Cholesterol: 0 mg
Fat: 0.3 g Fiber: 2.3 g Protein: 2.6 g Sodium: 7 mg

7. Delectable Meat Dishes

Unlike Western dishes, in which meat is often the focus, authentic Chinese meals generally feature fresh vegetables and grains. When meat is added to a dish, it is usually in small amounts either to enhance flavor or to add a bit of color. Such sparing use of meat and abundant use of vegetables translates into nutritious Chinese meals that, when properly prepared, can be very low in fat.

Before the days of tractors and other modern agricultural machinery, the Chinese used cattle as an affordable source of labor. Unlike cattle in the West, those in China were not raised as a source of food. As a result, beef and dairy products were not common ingredients in Chinese cuisine. Perhaps as a result of Western influence, Chinese interest in beef has increased over the years.

Skinless chicken and turkey are leaner than most cuts of beef and pork, making them valuable ingredients in low-fat dishes. (And the white-meat portions are even leaner than the dark ones.) Even beef and pork, although not as lean as skinless poultry, are both considerably leaner today than they were just a short while ago. For more information on the fat content, as well as the nutrients found in meats and poultry, see the section beginning on page 7.

Chicken is the most popular meat used in Chinese cooking. Low in fat, chicken can be cooked with almost any vegetable, and it can be substituted for the meat, fish, or seafood ingredients in most recipes

Turkey, which is not a traditional Chinese ingredient, is relatively low in fat and can be substituted for the chicken and the other meats in most dishes. Marinated in your favorite blend of Oriental spices, meaty turkey thighs can be steamed or baked and served with rice and fresh vegetables. Like chicken breast cutlets, turkey cutlets are ideal for stir-frying.

Although beef and pork are easily interchangeable, there are some differences between the two. First, when stir-fried, beef should be cooked very quickly over high heat, while pork should be cooked over medium heat for a slightly longer period of time. Overcooked beef loses its tenderness. Second, beef has a stronger, more definitive taste than pork. For this reason, beef holds up well with stronger-tasting vegetables such as green peppers, white onions, or leeks, as well as liberal amounts of ginger and garlic.

You may be surprised to discover how delicious and satisfying the following low-fat creations can be. Most are perfect served over a bed of rice or noodles, or alongside a serving of fresh vegetables. Remember, feel free to substitute your choice of meat or poultry for the ones listed.

When Dining Out

The recipes in this book show just how easy it is to prepare low-fat and fat-free Chinese-style dishes at home. Unfortunately, foods prepared in Chinese restaurants are a different story. Stir-fried and deep-fried dishes are characteristically heavy and oily. "Americanized" Chinese restaurants often use liberal portions of meat in their dishes, as well.

There are, however, things you can do to avoid this overload of fat when dining out. First of all, in an effort to satisfy health-conscious consumers, many Chinese restaurants now offer a variety of low-fat selections. And even when such selections are not offered, there are other strategies you can use to keep you within your fat budget. For instance:

❑ *Call ahead to the restaurant and inquire if special food-preparation requests—such as steaming or stir-frying with scant amounts of oil—are honored.*

❑ *When selecting items that are broiled or grilled, be sure to ask questions about the amount of fat used in their preparation. (Broiled and grilled items are often basted with flavorful oils as they cook.)*

❑ *Use low-fat sauces and seasonings to add a spark of flavor to otherwise bland dishes.*

❑ *Avoid all deep-fried menu items such as dumplings, wontons, and crispy noodles.*

❑ *Choose dishes such as steamed vegetables and plain rice. Add your own choice of seasonings for flavor.*

❑ *When ordering dumplings, choose those that are steamed—not fried.*

❑ *When choosing stir-fried dishes, request that very little oil be used in their preparation.*

❑ *When selecting dishes with chicken, request white-meat portions only. White meat is lower in fat than dark.*

❑ *Avoid ordering duck, which is very fatty.*

❑ *Watch what you drink. Both alcoholic and nonalcoholic cocktails are usually very high in calories. Drink tea instead.*

❑ *Remember that rice or noodles should be the meal's foundation. Meat and fish dishes should serve only as complements.*

❑ *If portions are large, as they often are in Chinese restaurants, split an entrée with a friend, or take half the entrée home. Most Chinese dishes reheat well and can be enjoyed the next day.*

Beef with Broccoli Nest

For a milder version of this dish, substitute 1 tablespoon honey mustard sauce and 2 teaspoons water for the chili pepper flakes. Be sure to slice the meat against the grain to insure tenderness.

1. Combine the marinade ingredients in a small bowl. Add the beef, toss to coat, and marinate in the refrigerator for at least 10 minutes.

2. To prepare the broccoli, first remove the florets and cut them in half lengthwise. Peel the tough outer skin from the stems, then cut the stems into $1/4$-inch slices. Set aside.

3. Combine the seasoning-blend ingredients in a small bowl and set aside.

4. Lightly coat a nonstick wok or frying pan with cooking spray and place over high heat. Add the marinated beef and stir-fry until the meat is no longer pink (about 1 minute). Remove to a bowl.

5. Recoat the pan with cooking spray and place over high heat. Add the broccoli and stir-fry until it turns bright green (3 to 4 minutes). Add the seasoning blend and cook another 2 minutes.

6. On a serving plate, form the steamed rice into the shape of a nest. Mound the beef in the center of the nest and arrange the broccoli on top of the rice and around the beef.

NUTRITIONAL FACTS (PER SERVING)
Calories: 124 Carbohydrates: 19.3 g Cholesterol: 18 mg
Fat: 1 g Fiber: 1.1 g Protein: 8.5 g Sodium: 69 mg

Yield: *6 servings*

12 ounces beef eye-of-round, cut into thin strips

1 pound fresh broccoli

3 cups steamed glutinous rice

MARINADE

2 tablespoons low-sodium soy sauce

1 tablespoon fresh lemon juice

$1^{1}/2$ teaspoons cornstarch

$1/2$ teaspoon rice vinegar

SEASONING BLEND

3 tablespoons fresh lemon juice

1 tablespoon rice wine

2 teaspoons minced fresh ginger

$1/4$ teaspoon chili pepper flakes

Shredded Szechuan Pork

Yield: 6 servings

12 ounces lean pork, cut into thin strips

4 shiitake mushroom caps, thinly sliced (if using dried variety, *see* hydrating instructions on page 37)

1 cup coarsely grated cucumber

1 cup thinly sliced red bell peppers

2 tablespoons minced fresh garlic

2 tablespoons minced fresh ginger

2 green onions, chopped

MARINADE

1 tablespoon low-sodium soy sauce

1 teaspoon cornstarch

1 tablespoon rice wine

SEASONING BLEND

1 tablespoon rice vinegar

1 tablespoon low-sodium soy sauce

1/2 teaspoon ground black pepper

1/4 teaspoon chili pepper flakes

1. Combine the marinade ingredients in a large bowl. Add the pork, toss to coat, and marinate at room temperature for 20 minutes.

2. Combine the seasoning-blend ingredients in a small bowl and set aside.

3. Lightly coat a nonstick wok or frying pan with cooking spray and place over medium heat. Add the garlic and ginger and sauté until the garlic begins to brown.

4. Add the pork and marinade. Stir-fry the pork until no pink remains (about 2 minutes). Add the mushrooms, cucumber, bell pepper, and seasoning blend. Continue to stir-fry another 2 minutes.

5. Transfer to a serving bowl, garnish with green onions, and serve over rice.

NUTRITIONAL FACTS (PER SERVING)

Calories: 100 Carbohydrates: 6 g Cholesterol: 25 mg
Fat: 2.5 g Fiber: 1.1 g Protein: 10.2 g Sodium: 92 mg

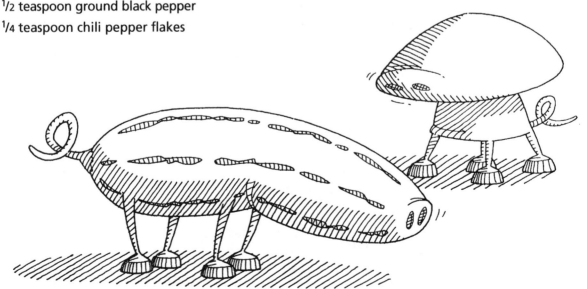

Bai Zai Chicken

This exotic dish, which is very popular in southern China, makes a great appetizer.

Yield: *5 servings*

1. Place the chicken breasts in a large pot with enough water to cover and bring to a rolling boil. Cook for 20 minutes. Remove the chicken, allow to cool, then slice into long strips.

2. Mix the dipping sauce ingredients together in a small bowl.

3. Place the bowl of dipping sauce in the center of a serving plate and surround with the chicken strips.

4. Dip a strip in the sauce and enjoy.

16 ounces skinless, boneless chicken breasts

DIPPING SAUCE

2 tablespoons low-sodium soy sauce

1 tablespoon fresh lemon juice

1 tablespoon rice vinegar

1/2 teaspoon sesame oil

4 cloves garlic, crushed

1 tablespoon minced fresh ginger

1/2 teaspoon chili pepper flakes

1 sprig fresh cilantro, minced

NUTRITIONAL FACTS (PER SERVING)

Calories: 125 Carbohydrates: 1.1 g Cholesterol: 57 mg
Fat: 2.8 g Fiber: 0.1 g Protein: 21 g Sodium: 206 mg

Curried Beef Rolls

1. Mix all of the filling ingredients together in a medium bowl.

2. Lightly coat a nonstick wok or frying pan with cooking spray and place over medium-high heat. Add the beef mixture and sauté until the beef is no longer pink (3 to 5 minutes). Mix in the sesame oil.

3. Mound the beef in the middle of a serving platter and surround it with the lettuce leaves. Place 2 tablespoons of beef on the center of a leaf, wrap it up, and eat the filled roll taco-style.

Yield: *20 appetizer-sized rolls*

20 butter lettuce leaves

FILLING

12 ounces extra-lean ground beef

3 large cloves garlic, minced

1 tablespoon minced fresh ginger

1 green onion, chopped

1 cup finely chopped white onion

2 tablespoons rice wine

2 tablespoons low-sodium soy sauce

2 tablespoons curry paste, or
1 tablespoon powder

2 teaspoons cornstarch

1 teaspoon sesame oil

NUTRITIONAL FACTS (PER ROLL)

Calories: 42 Carbohydrates: 1.5 g Cholesterol: 9 mg
Fat: 2.4 g Fiber: 0.3g Protein: 2.4 g Sodium: 31 mg

Pineapple Bowls with Chicken

Yield: 2 filled pineapple halves

1 large pineapple, halved length-wise

FILLING

4 ounces cooked chicken breast strips (*see* page 9)

1/2 cup each, red, green, and yellow bell peppers, thinly sliced

2 tablespoons fat-free Italian-style salad dressing

1 tablespoon fresh lemon juice

1 teaspoon minced fresh ginger

1/2 teaspoon Eden Foods sesame shake, or chopped sesame seeds

The combination of chicken and colorful bell peppers served in pineapple shells makes this festive dish perfect for special occasions.

1. Carefully scrape the pineapple from the halves and reserve the shells to use as bowls. Shred the pineapple and set aside.

2. Lightly coat a nonstick wok or frying pan with cooking spray and place over medium heat. Add the pineapple and bell peppers, and sauté until the peppers start to soften.

3. Add the chicken, salad dressing, lemon juice, and ginger to the pan. Mix the ingredients thoroughly.

4. Dividing the filling evenly, fill the pineapple shells. Garnish with sesame shake and serve.

NUTRITIONAL FACTS (PER PINEAPPLE HALF)

Calories: 140 Carbohydrates: 24.7 g Cholesterol: 18 mg
Fat: 2.2 g Fiber: 3.3 g Protein: 8.3 g Sodium: 135 mg

Lemony Chicken Salad

Yield: 4 servings

3 cups coarsely grated celery

1 cup cooked chicken breast strips (*see* page 9)

2 tablespoons shredded ham

SAUCE

1/3 cup low-sodium fat-free chicken broth

3 tablespoons fresh lemon juice

2 tablespoons light corn syrup

2 tablespoons rice vinegar

1 tablespoon grated lemon peel

3 cloves garlic, minced

1. Combine all of the sauce ingredients in a small bowl.

2. Arrange the shredded celery on a serving plate. Add a layer of chicken strips, and top with a sprinkling of ham.

3. Spoon the sauce on the salad and serve.

NUTRITIONAL FACTS (PER SERVING)

Calories: 134 Carbohydrates: 14 g Cholesterol: 38.6 mg
Fat: 2 g Fiber: 2 g Protein: 15.5 g Sodium: 234 mg

Four-Spice Pork with Spinach

The ginger, garlic, green onions, and chili make a wonderfully hot and tasty combination. This dish can stand on its own or serve as a topping for boiled noodles or steamed rice.

1. Remove the stems from the spinach leaves. Cut the stems into 2-inch lengths and cut any large leaves in half.

2. Combine the marinade ingredients in a small bowl. Add the pork, toss to coat, and marinate in the refrigerator for at least 10 minutes.

3. Bring 4 cups of water to boil in a large pot. Add the spinach and blanch until the leaves are bright green (do not overcook). Drain and set aside.

4. Lightly coat a nonstick wok or frying pan with cooking spray and place over medium heat. Add the garlic, ginger, and chili flakes, and sauté until the garlic begins to brown.

5. Add the pork and marinade, and stir-fry until the pork is no longer pink (about 2 minutes). Add the spinach and toss with the other ingredients. Cook another minute.

6. Transfer to a serving bowl and sprinkle with sesame oil. Garnish with green onion and serve.

Yield: *6 servings*

12 ounces pork tenderloin, thinly sliced

2 1/2 pounds fresh spinach, thoroughly washed

2 tablespoons minced fresh ginger

4 cloves garlic, crushed

1/2 teaspoon chili pepper flakes

2 green onions, minced

1/2 teaspoon sesame oil

MARINADE

2 tablespoons low-sodium soy sauce or teriyaki sauce

2 teaspoons fresh lemon juice

1 1/2 teaspoons rice vinegar

1 teaspoon cornstarch

NUTRITIONAL FACTS (PER SERVING)

Calories: 108 Carbohydrates: 8.4 g Cholesterol: 26 mg
Fat: 2.5 g Fiber: 5.3 g Protein: 14.1 g Sodium: 237 mg

Beef with Ginger and Pineapple

Yield: 6 servings

12 ounces beef bottom round, cut into thin strips

3 cups bite-sized pineapple cubes

2 tablespoons minced fresh ginger

1/2 teaspoon Eden Foods sesame shake, or chopped sesame seeds

1/2 teaspoon Mrs. Dash extra-spicy seasoning

2 tablespoons water

2 green onions, cut into 3-inch lengths

MARINADE

2 tablespoons fresh lemon juice

1 tablespoon low-sodium soy sauce

1 tablespoon cooking wine

2 teaspoons cornstarch

1. Combine the marinade ingredients in a large bowl. Add the beef strips, toss to coat, and marinate in the refrigerator for 1 hour.

2. Lightly coat a nonstick wok or frying pan with cooking spray and place over high heat. Add the beef along with the marinade, and stir-fry the beef until no pink remains (about 1 minute.) Remove from the pan and set aside.

3. Recoat the pan with cooking spray and reduce the heat to medium. Add the pineapple and ginger, and sauté until heated through.

4. Add the cooked beef to the pan along with the sesame shake, Mrs. Dash seasoning, and 2 tablespoons of water. Mix all of the ingredients together well and cook another 2 minutes. Stir in the green onions and transfer to a serving bowl.

5. Serve hot over a bed of rice.

NUTRITIONAL FACTS (PER SERVING)

Calories: 126 Carbohydrates: 11.3 g Cholesterol: 33 mg
Fat: 2.7 g Fiber: 1.2 g Protein: 12.7 g Sodium: 96 mg

Chinese Cooking—Cantonese Style

The Southeastern region of China is famous for the Cantonese style of cooking. European trade with the Orient began at the seaport of Canton, which became the gateway to the West. The Cantonese soon emigrated to Europe and America, where they established the first Chinese-style restaurants. This is why the majority of Chinese restaurants in Europe and the United States are Cantonese.

The Cantonese cooking style blends the natural flavors of individual ingredients in a dish. Soy sauce, hoison sauce, plum sauce, ginger, and wine are the main seasonings used. This cooking style specializes in stir-frying and steaming, and commonly uses chicken stock as a cooking medium. It is also noted for dishes that include meat, poultry, fish, and shellfish. Fried rice accompanies most dishes. Beef with Ginger and Pineapple, above, and Pumpkin Chicken Pot on page 110 are delicious low-fat versions of Cantonese-style dishes.

Steamed Turkey Cakes

For a spark of heat, add $1/2$ teaspoon of chili pepper flakes to the patty mixture.

1. Combine all of the patty-mixture ingredients in a large bowl. Mix well and divide the mixture into 6 patties. Set aside.

2. Cut the cabbage leaves into circles that are as large as the patties.

3. Arrange the leaves on a steamer plate, and place the patties on top.

4. Steam over high heat for 10 to 12 minutes, then reduce the heat to medium and steam another 8 to 10 minutes.

5. Transfer the "cakes" to a serving platter and garnish with cilantro. Serve plain or with one of the dipping sauces in Chapter 3.

Yield: 6 cakes

6 large cabbage leaves

3 sprigs fresh cilantro, minced

PATTY MIXTURE

8 ounces extra-lean ground turkey

8 ounces finely chopped water chestnuts

2 green onions, finely chopped

2 tablespoons minced fresh ginger

2 tablespoons cornstarch

1 tablespoon low-sodium soy sauce

2 teaspoons rice wine vinegar

1 teaspoon Mrs. Dash seasoning

$1/2$ teaspoon sesame oil

NUTRITIONAL FACTS (PER CAKE)

Calories: 96 Carbohydrates: 12.5 g Cholesterol: 14 mg
Fat: 0.9 g Fiber: 0.7 g Protein: 7.7 g Sodium: 60 mg

Mu Shu Chicken

Yield: *8 mu shu pancakes*

8 white flour tortilla shells (10 inch)

2 tablespoons mustard sauce

FILLING

8 ounces cooked chicken breast strips (page 9)

4 shiitake mushroom caps, sliced (if using dried variety, *see* hydrating instructions on page 37)

1 cup egg substitute

8 ounces water chestnuts, coarsely chopped

1 tablespoon minced fresh ginger

4 green onions, minced

SAUCE

1 cup low-sodium fat-free chicken broth

2 tablespoons low-sodium ketchup

2 tablespoons rice vinegar

I have found tortilla shells to be the perfect "pancakes" for this flavorful chicken. You can fill the tortillas and roll them up before serving or let everyone fill their own.

1. Combine the sauce ingredients in a small bowl.

2. Lightly coat a nonstick wok or frying pan with cooking spray and place over medium heat. Add half the egg substitute and cook on both sides to form a thin pancake. Remove to a plate and cook the remaining egg substitute. Cut both pancakes into thin strips and set aside.

3. Recoat the pan with cooking spray. Add the mushrooms and water chestnuts, and stir-fry until the mushrooms begin to soften (1 to 2 minutes).

4. Add the chicken, egg, ginger, and sauce mixture. Cook until the liquid is absorbed (2 to 3 minutes). Transfer to a serving bowl and sprinkle with green onions.

5. Spread a little mustard sauce on a tortilla shell, then place 3 tablespoons of filling in the center. Fold the right and left sides of the tortilla shell over the filling, then roll up the shell to form a neat packet.

NUTRITIONAL FACTS (PER PANCAKE)

Calories: 187 Carbohydrates: 30.7 g Cholesterol: 9 mg
Fat: 2.4 g Fiber: 0.6 g Protein: 9.3 g Sodium: 154 mg

Chinese Cooking—Peking Style

Located in the northeast region of China, Peking—the site of the Imperial Palace and the country's intellectual and cultural center—has always attracted the finest chefs. Until the seventeenth century, Peking was considered the gourmet capital of China. Huge, lavish feasts held at the Imperial Court are reputed to have been nothing less than magnificent. Sometimes these extravagant meals took days to consume.

Regional Peking cooking is known for its light, elegant, mildly seasoned foods. Characteristically, it employs the liberal use of garlic, scallions, leeks, and chives. The dishes most commonly associated with this cooking school are Peking duck, mu shu pork and chicken, and boiled dumplings. Some examples of low-fat Peking-style dishes in this book include Spinach-Topped Noodles on page 74 and Mu Shu Chicken, above.

Top Left: Spinach-Topped Noodles (page 74)
Right: Pumpkin Chicken Pot (page 110)
Bottom Left: Three Threads Tofu (page 86)

Top Right: Beef with Broccoli Nest (page 101)
Left: Pineapple Bowl with Chicken (page 104)
Bottom Right: Ma Po's Tofu (page 89)

Sweet-and-Sour Pork

1. Combine the marinade ingredients in a bowl. Add the pork, toss to coat, and marinate in the refrigerator for 30 minutes.

2. In another small bowl, combine the sauce ingredients and mix well. Set aside.

3. Lightly coat a nonstick wok or frying pan with cooking spray and place over medium-high heat. Add the pork and stir-fry until it is no longer pink (3 to 4 minutes). Transfer the pork to a bowl and set aside.

4. Recoat the pan with cooking spray and reduce the heat to medium. Add the bell pepper and onion, and sauté until they begin to soften (2 to 3 minutes).

5. Return the cooked pork to the pan along with pineapple and sauce. Bring the ingredients to a boil, then remove the pan from the heat.

6. Serve hot over rice.

NUTRITIONAL FACTS (PER SERVING)
Calories: 154 Carbohydrates: 15.7 g Cholesterol: 43 mg
Fat: 2.5 g Fiber: 1.5 g Protein: 15.1 g Sodium: 188 mg

Yield: *4 servings*

12 ounces pork tenderloin, cut into thin strips

1 cup bite-sized pineapple cubes*

1 cup thinly sliced green bell pepper

1 cup thinly sliced white onion

MARINADE

2 tablespoons rice vinegar

2 tablespoons low-sodium soy sauce

2 tablespoons minced fresh ginger

SAUCE

1/2 cup pineapple juice

1 tablespoon low-sodium soy sauce

1 tablespoon rice vinegar

2 teaspoons cornstarch

* If using canned pineapple, reserve the juice for the sauce.

Pumpkin Chicken Pot

Yield: 6 servings

5 pound pumpkin

4 ounces skinless chicken breasts, cut into cubes

5 shiitake mushroom caps, chopped (if using dried variety, *see* hydrating instructions on page 37)

2 teaspoons minced fresh garlic

1½ teaspoons minced fresh ginger

4 cups low-sodium fat-free chicken broth

2 cups Rice Dream beverage, or reduced-fat soymilk

1 tablespoon fresh lemon juice

2 teaspoons rice vinegar

4 sprigs fresh cilantro, minced

This dish, which is served in a pumpkin shell, always delights my American friends, who generally think of pumpkins as either Halloween decor or filling for Thanksgiving pies. The pumpkin meat on the inner shell lends a warm, mellow flavor to the other ingredients. And don't forget to roast the seeds as an added treat.

1. Using a sharp knife, cut the top off the pumpkin. Scoop out the seeds and stringy pulp. Set aside.

2. Lightly coat a nonstick wok or frying pan with cooking spray and place over medium heat. Add the garlic and ginger, and sauté until the garlic begins to brown (about 3 minutes). Add the chicken and mushrooms, and sauté until the chicken is no longer pink and the mushrooms are soft (3 to 5 minutes).

3. Add the broth, Rice Dream, lemon juice, and vinegar to the pan and mix with the other ingredients. Pour into the pumpkin shell.

4. Put the lid back on the pumpkin and place in a steamer set over boiling water until the pumpkin shell begins to soften (30 to 35 minutes).

5. Set the pumpkin on a platter, remove the lid, and garnish with cilantro. Ladle the stew directly from the pumpkin into serving bowls.

NUTRITIONAL FACTS (PER SERVING)

Calories: 109 Carbohydrates: 17.5 g Cholesterol: 6 mg
Fat: 0.9 g Fiber: 2.2 g Protein: 5.4 g Sodium: 78 mg

Kung Po Beef

1. Combine the sauce ingredients in a bowl and set aside.

2. Lightly coat a nonstick wok or frying pan with cooking spray and place over medium heat. Add the garlic and ginger, and sauté until the garlic begins to brown.

3. Increase the heat to high, add the beef, and stir-fry until the beef is no longer pink (about 1 minute.) Remove from the pan and set aside.

4. Recoat the pan with cooking spray. Add the bell peppers and chili peppers, and stir-fry for 2 minutes.

5. Return the cooked beef to the pan, mix with the other ingredients, and cook another minute. Stir in the sauce and green onions.

6. Garnish with peanuts before serving.

NUTRITIONAL FACTS (PER SERVING)

Calories: 132 Carbohydrates: 6.7 g Cholesterol: 38 mg
Fat: 3 g Fiber: 1.1 g Protein: 17.5 g Sodium: 40 mg

Yield: *5 servings*

12 ounces beef eye-of-round, cut into thin strips

1 cup thinly sliced red bell pepper

1 cup thinly sliced green bell pepper

2 hot green chili peppers, thinly sliced

6 green onions (white bulb only), thinly sliced

4 cloves garlic, crushed

1 teaspoon minced fresh ginger

$\frac{1}{2}$ teaspoon ground white pepper

SAUCE

2 teaspoons chopped roasted peanuts (*see* Roasting Nuts on page 62)

2 tablespoons low-sodium soy sauce

2 teaspoons cornstarch

1 tablespoon rice wine

8. Seafood Extravaganza

Fish and shellfish have always been popular ingredients in Chinese cooking. Traditionally served on New Year's Eve, fish signifies a wish for good fortune during the year to come. *Yu*, the Chinese word for fish, means "more than enough." At most family gatherings and festive occasions, fish is traditionally served at the meal's end, where it is enjoyed but not completely eaten. The leftover fish signifies that there is more for the next year.

The good news about fish is that it is a healthy food choice. Many fish—cod, halibut, and sole, for example—are nearly fat-free. And although other varieties may be moderately fatty, they provide essential omega-3 fatty acids. These acids are valuable because they help reduce blood cholesterol, lower blood pressure, and prevent the formation of dangerous blood clots. Also, most fish and shellfish (with the exception of shrimp) are low in cholesterol. And all seafood, including shellfish, is very low in saturated fat.

I have attended many dinner parties since moving to the United States, but fish has never been served at any of them. Often I have heard my friends complain of the fishy taste and smell of most seafood. This signifies a lack of freshness. As fish is very perishable, it is important to choose fresh products only. When shopping for whole fish, choose ones with clear eyes, red gills, and shiny skin. When buying fish fillets, be sure the flesh is firm and has a clean seaweed odor. Choose fresh shrimp that are white or gray in color. Never buy shrimp that smell like ammonia; this signifies spoilage.

One Labor Day, I served a whole salmon to guests and was thrilled as I watched the fish rapidly disappear! I guess my friends do love fish after all; that is, when it is properly prepared by a "master" Chinese cook.

Along with choosing only fresh products, there is another secret to my seafood-cooking success—I always use fresh ginger, wine, vinegar, and lemon juice to complement the flavor. Without these seasonings, I feel as if the dish is incomplete, like a half-painted portrait.

When testing for doneness, insert a clean fork into the thickest part of the fish. The fish is done if the flesh is no longer translucent and it flakes easily.

You will find a wide variety of fabulous low-fat fish and shellfish dishes—both entrées and appetizers—on the following pages. Each dish is savory and delicious. Why not surprise your family with a special dinner of Sautéed Shrimp with Snow Peas or Scallops with Orange Sauce? Or impress them with one of the sensational baked or broiled fish fillet entrées. On those special occasions when you are entertaining guests, grace your buffet table with a Whole Baked Salmon. Covered in a scallion garnish, it makes a most impressive centerpiece.

Rescuing a Dish

One of the tips provided below may help you to save an otherwise failed dish:

• *If the food is too salty,*

try adding a little vinegar or sugar to counterbalance the saltiness. Cornstarch dissolved in a little water then added to the mixture is another solution. You can also add more vegetables, even frozen ones, to reduce some of the salty flavor.

• *If the food is too sour—has too much vinegar,*

a pinch of salt will help counterbalance the sourness of the dish and improve its taste.

• *If the food is too bland,*

simply adding a dash of soy sauce, chili oil, or lemon juice will help to liven it up. You may also consider using herbs or spices such as garlic or black pepper to help enhance the food's flavor.

• *If the sauce is too thick,*

stir in a little cold water while the sauce is still simmering. The amount of water added will depend upon the amount of sauce that is present and how thick it is. Begin with a tablespoon or two and continue adding water as needed.

• *If the sauce is too thin,*

combine approximately 1 teaspoon of cornstarch with 1 tablespoon of water. Stir the mixture until the cornstarch is dissolved, then add it to the sauce. Stir the sauce for a few minutes until it begins to thicken. If necessary, repeat this procedure.

• *If the dish is overcooked,*

some lightly cooked carrots, peas, water chestnuts, or snow peas can be added for texture and color.

Whole Baked Salmon

This dish makes a great centerpiece for special dinner parties. It is easy to prepare and can feed a group of ten or more. I try to choose a fish that will just fit into my largest baking pan. (I prefer to cook the entire fish, but you may opt to remove the head and tail before cooking.) For optimal flavor, allow the salmon to marinate overnight.

1. Combine the marinade ingredients in a pan and set aside. (Be sure the pan is big enough to hold the fish.)

2. Cut 3 to 4 quarter-inch-deep diagonal slashes along both sides of the fish. Fill these slashes, as well as the cleaned inside of the fish with ginger and garlic.

3. Place the fish in the marinade, turn to coat, and refrigerate 24 hours. Every few hours, turn the fish over and spoon some of the marinade on top and inside.

4. Reserving the marinade, transfer the fish to a nonstick baking pan that has been lightly coated with cooking spray.

5. Place the pan on a low rack and broil the fish until the skin turns golden brown (about 15 minutes). Turn the fish over and broil the other side. To test for doneness, stick a clean fork into the thickest part of the fish. If the flesh is no longer translucent and flakes easily, it is done.

6. Turn off the heat, but leave the cooked salmon in the oven to stay warm.

7. Lightly coat a nonstick wok or frying pan with cooking spray and place over medium-high heat. Add the broccoli and cauliflower and stir-fry for 5 minutes. Add the Mrs. Dash seasoning and the reserved marinade, and mix thoroughly. Cook another 3 to 5 minutes.

8. Transfer the salmon to a serving dish and surround it with the stir-fried vegetables. Garnish with green onion and cilantro and serve.

Yield: *14 servings*

5-pound whole salmon, cleaned and scaled

3 cups broccoli florets

3 cups cauliflower florets

1/4 cup minced fresh garlic

1/4 cup minced fresh ginger

1 teaspoon Mrs. Dash extra-spicy seasoning

3 green onions, chopped

3 sprigs cilantro, chopped

MARINADE

1/2 cup water

1/2 cup low-sodium teriyaki sauce

1/4 cup fresh lemon juice

3 tablespoons rice vinegar

2 tablespoons cooking wine

1 teaspoon five-spice powder

1 teaspoon chili pepper flakes

1 teaspoon ground black pepper

NUTRITIONAL FACTS (PER SERVING)
Calories: 158 Carbohydrates: 5.4 g Cholesterol: 35 mg
Fat: 5.6 g Fiber: 1.2 g Protein: 25.4 g Sodium: 165 mg

Shrimp Cake

Yield: 9-inch-square cake

12 ounces raw shrimp, peeled and deveined

16 ounces firm low-fat tofu

1/4 cup minced green onion

2 egg whites

2 tablespoons cornstarch

1 tablespoon fresh lemon juice

1/2 teaspoon sesame oil

1/2 teaspoon ground white pepper

1. Preheat the oven to 375°F. Lightly coat a 9-inch square baking pan with cooking spray and set aside.

2. Rinse the shrimp with cold water, pat dry, and cut into small pieces the size of corn kernels. Set aside

3. Place all of the ingredients in a blender and blend into a paste.

4. Spoon the mixture into the baking pan and spread it evenly. Bake for 20 to 25 minutes. To check for doneness, insert a fork in the center of the cake. If the fork comes out clean, the cake is done.

5. Allow the cake to cool about 3 minutes. Cut it into 3-inch squares and serve.

NUTRITIONAL FACTS (PER 3-INCH SQUARE)
Calories: 154 Carbohydrates: 5.5 g Cholesterol: 104 mg
Fat: 3.1 g Fiber: 0.3 g Protein: 23.8 g Sodium: 236 mg

Lemon Fish

Yield: 4 servings

1 1/2 pounds sole, catfish, or pollock fillets

1 small white onion, thinly sliced

5 sprigs cilantro, chopped

SEASONING BLEND

1/4 cup fresh lemon juice

2 tablespoons fat-free cream cheese

1 teaspoon ground white pepper

1/2 teaspoon Mrs. Dash extra-spicy seasoning

2 bay leaves, crushed

1. Preheat the oven to 350°F. Coat a baking pan with cooking spray and set aside.

2. Lightly coat a nonstick frying pan with cooking spray and place over medium heat. Add the onion and sauté until soft (2 to 3 minutes).

3. Combine the seasoning-blend ingredients and cooked onion in a small bowl.

4. Place the fish fillets in a single layer in the baking pan and top with the seasoning-blend mixture. Bake until the fish easily flakes with a fork (15 to 20 minutes).

5. Transfer the fillets to a platter, garnish with cilantro, and serve with rice and fresh vegetables.

NUTRITIONAL FACTS (PER SERVING)
Calories: 123 Carbohydrates: 4.2 g Cholesterol: 55 mg
Fat: 1.5 g Fiber: 0.6 g Protein: 22.4 g Sodium: 114 mg

Squid with Garlic Sauce

1. To make the sauce, combine the cornstarch and broth in a small bowl, then add the remaining sauce ingredients. Mix well and set aside.

2. Lightly coat a nonstick wok or frying pan with cooking spray and place over medium heat. Add the garlic, and sauté until the garlic begins to brown. Add the squid and cook until it turns white 2 to 3 minutes). Transfer to a bowl.

3. Increase the heat to high, add the mushrooms and cabbage, and stir-fry for 1 to 2 minutes. Return the squid to the pan along with the sauce and reduce the heat to low. Cover and simmer until the squid is soft (5 to 6 minutes).

4. Transfer the ingredients to a serving bowl and sprinkle with sesame oil. Arrange the green onion pieces artistically on top and serve hot.

NUTRITIONAL FACTS (PER SERVING)
Calories: 122 Carbohydrates: 8.8 g Cholesterol: 215 mg
Fat: 1.9 g Fiber: 1.1 g Protein: 15.9 g Sodium: 189 mg

Yield: 5 servings

$1^{1}/_{2}$ pounds fresh squid, cleaned and cut into 1-inch-wide strips

5 cloves garlic, chopped

6 shiitake mushroom caps, sliced (if using dried variety, see hydrating instructions on page 37)

12 ounces Napa cabbage, cut into 2-x-$^{3}/_{4}$ -inch pieces

4 green onions (white part only), cut into 1-inch pieces

$^{1}/_{2}$ teaspoon sesame oil

SAUCE

1 teaspoon cornstarch

1 cup low-sodium fat-free chicken broth

2 tablespoons low-sodium soy sauce

1 tablespoon cooking wine

1 teaspoon Eden Foods sesame shake, or chopped sesame seeds

$^{1}/_{2}$ teaspoon chili pepper flakes

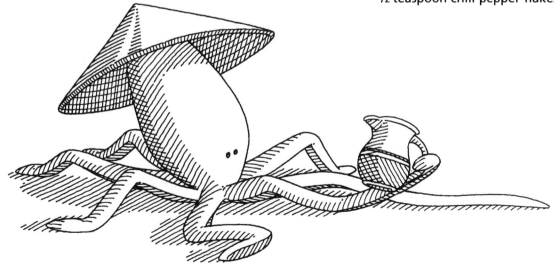

Baked Yogurt Fish

Yield: *4 servings*

1½ pounds sole, catfish, or pollock
fillets

2 green onions, chopped

SEASONING BLEND

1 cup plain fat-free yogurt

1½ teaspoon fresh lemon juice

5 cloves garlic, minced

1 teaspoon white pepper

1. Preheat the oven to 350°F. Coat a nonstick baking pan with cooking spray and set aside.

2. Combine the seasoning-blend ingredients in a small bowl and set aside.

3. Place the fish fillets in a single layer in the baking pan and top with the seasoning-blend mixture. Bake until the fish easily flakes with a fork (15 to 20 minutes).

4. Transfer the fillets to a platter, garnish with green onions, and serve with rice and fresh vegetables.

NUTRITIONAL FACTS (PER SERVING)

Calories: 122 Carbohydrates: 4.9 g Cholesterol: 47 mg
Fat: 1.3 g Fiber: 0.2 g Protein: 22 g Sodium: 121 mg

Baked Sole with Tomatoes

Yield: *4 servings*

1½ pounds sole, catfish, or pollock
fillets

4 plum tomatoes, cut into 1-inch
cubes

5 sprigs cilantro, chopped

MARINADE

3 tablespoons fresh lemon juice

2 teaspoons cooking wine

2 tablespoons extra-hot mustard
sauce

1 teaspoon rice vinegar

1 teaspoons ground white pepper

½ teaspoon Mrs. Dash Seasoning

5 bay leaves, crushed

5 cloves garlic, minced

1. Combine the marinade ingredients in a bowl. Add the fish fillets and marinate at room temperature for 30 minutes (or several hours in the refrigerator).

2. Preheat the oven to 350°F. Lightly coat a nonstick baking pan with cooking spray.

3. Place the marinated fish in a single layer in the baking pan and top with the marinade and tomatoes. Bake until the fish easily flakes with a fork (15 to 20 minutes).

4. Transfer the fillets to a platter, garnish with cilantro, and serve.

NUTRITIONAL FACTS (PER SERVING)

Calories: 128 Carbohydrates: 8.1 g Cholesterol: 47 mg
Fat: 1.5 g Fiber: 1.5 g Protein: 20.3 g Sodium: 121 mg

Smelts in Five-Spice Sauce

This dish makes a great appetizer, as well as a main dish served with rice and vegetables.

1. Arrange the smelts in a nonstick baking dish that has been lightly coated with cooking spray. Add a little spray to the top of the fish and place in the broiler on a low rack. Cook until their skin begins to brown (about 5 minutes). Remove the smelts from the broiler, turn them over, and spray with a little more cooking spray (never use the spray near the flames of a broiler).

2. Return the smelts to the broiler and cook until their skin is light brown and their flesh is white and flaky (about 5 minutes).

3. To make the sauce, combine the cornstarch and water in a small pot, then mix in the remaining sauce ingredients. Heat until the sauce thickens.

4. Arrange the smelts on a serving platter and spoon the sauce on top. Garnish with green onions and cilantro and serve.

Yield: 5 servings

2 pounds fresh smelts, cleaned and patted dry

2 sprigs cilantro, chopped

1 green onion, chopped

SAUCE

1 teaspoon cornstarch

2 tablespoons water

2 tablespoons fresh lemon juice

1 teaspoon cooking wine

5 cloves garlic, crushed

2 teaspoons minced fresh ginger

1 teaspoon five-spice powder

1/2 teaspoon ground black pepper

NUTRITIONAL FACTS (PER SERVING)
Calories: 131 Carbohydrates: 3.7 g Cholesterol: 83 mg
Fat: 3 g Fiber: 0.4 g Protein: 21.4 g Sodium: 86 mg

Steamed Sea Bass in Wine Sauce

Yield: *4 servings*

1 1/2 pounds sea bass fillets

1 teaspoon minced fresh ginger

2 green onions, chopped

1/2 teaspoon sesame oil

SAUCE

1 tablespoon fresh lemon juice

1 1/2 teaspoons cooking wine

2 teaspoons low-sodium soy sauce

1 teaspoon rice vinegar

1/8 teaspoon chili pepper flakes

Trout and other firm-fleshed fish are also good choices for this recipe. And you can use the whole fish instead of fillets. For stronger flavor, marinate the fish in the sauce for 20 to 30 minutes before cooking.

1. Combine the sauce ingredients in a small bowl and set aside.

2. Cut 1/4-inch-deep diagonal slashes about 1/2-inch apart on one side of each fillet. Fill the slashes with the ginger and half of the green onion.

3. Arrange the fillets on a heat-resistant plate, cover with the sauce, and place in a steamer set over boiling water. Steam the fish until the flesh is white and flaky (about 15 minutes).

4. Transfer the fillets to a serving platter, sprinkle with sesame oil and the remaining green onion, and serve with rice and vegetables.

NUTRITIONAL FACTS (PER SERVING)
Calories: 134 Carbohydrates: 1 g Cholesterol: 52 mg
Fat: 3.1 g Fiber: 0.2 g Protein: 23.8 g Sodium: 144 mg

Regional Shanghai Cooking

Located in the eastern region of China, Shanghai is the country's largest and most famous seaport. Being a great cosmopolitan city and commercial center, Shanghai cooking has come to reflect the styles of many regions. This area's cooking depends largely on soy sauce, and uses a great deal of sugar. Its dishes popularly include fresh seafood—especially fresh-water shrimp—bamboo shoots, and pork. Rice is the staple. Try the Sautéed Shrimp with Snow Peas on page 121 and the Sweet-and-Sour Pork on page 109. They are delicious low-fat examples of Shanghai cooking.

Sautéed Shrimp with Snow Peas

For a spicier version of this dish, add 1 teaspoon of chili paste or oil.

Yield: *5 servings*

1. Rinse the shrimp with cold water and pat dry.

2. Combine the marinade ingredients in a bowl. Add the shrimp and marinate in the refrigerator for 30 minutes.

3. Lightly coat a nonstick wok or frying pan with cooking spray and place over medium heat. Reserving the marinade, add the shrimp and sauté until they just turn pink (2 to 3 minutes). Transfer to a bowl.

4. Add the snow peas, onion, and ginger to the pan and stir-fry for 1 to 2 minutes.

5. Add the reserved marinade and soy sauce to the pan along with the cooked shrimp. Mix the ingredients well and continue to cook until the most of the sauce is absorbed (1 to 2 minutes).

6. Transfer to a serving bowl, sprinkle with sesame oil, and serve hot.

1 pound raw shrimp, peeled and deveined

2 cups fresh snow peas

1 green onion, chopped

1 tablespoon minced fresh ginger

2 tablespoons low-sodium soy sauce

¼ teaspoon sesame oil

MARINADE

1 tablespoon cooking wine

1 teaspoon fresh lemon juice

¼ teaspoon Mrs. Dash seasoning

2 teaspoons cornstarch

NUTRITIONAL FACTS (PER SERVING)

Calories: 125 Carbohydrates: 8.4 g Cholesterol: 108 mg
Fat: 1.4 g Fiber: 3.1 g Protein: 16.7 g Sodium: 222 mg

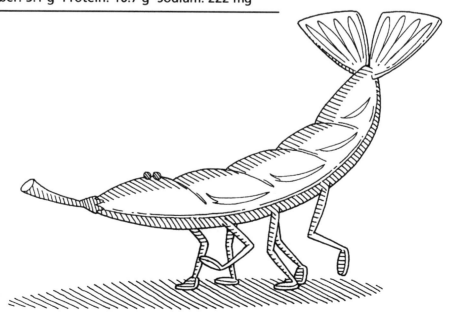

Broiled Salmon Fillets

Yield: 5 servings

1½ pounds salmon fillets

½ teaspoon Eden Foods sesame shake, or chopped sesame seeds

SAUCE

2 tablespoons fresh lemon juice

1 tablespoon low-sodium soy sauce

1 tablespoon rice vinegar

1 tablespoon cooking wine

¼ teaspoon chili pepper flakes

1. Combine the sauce ingredients in a small bowl and set aside.

2. Cut ¼-inch-deep diagonal slashes on one side of each fillet. Place the fillets on a broiling pan that has been lightly coated with cooking spray. Cover the fish with half the sauce.

3. Broil the fillets for 5 minutes, then turn them over. Spoon on the remaining sauce and broil until the fish easily flakes with a fork (about 5 minutes).

4. Transfer the cooked fillets to a platter, sprinkle with sesame shake, and serve hot with vegetables and rice.

NUTRITIONAL FACTS (PER SERVING)

Calories: 112 Carbohydrates: 0.7 g Cholesterol: 28 mg
Fat: 4.2 g Fiber: 0.1 g Protein: 19.9 g Sodium: 109 mg

Three-Color Balls

Yield: 20 shrimp balls

16 ounces raw shrimp, peeled and deveined

8 ounces watermelon

8 ounces honeydew melon

1 teaspoon minced fresh ginger

½ teaspoon sesame oil

½ teaspoon cooking wine

1 teaspoon cornstarch

½ teaspoon ground white pepper

½ teaspoon Eden Foods sesame shake, or chopped sesame seeds

This is a wonderful summer appetizer. For an even more creative presentation, place the balls on a bed of thinly sliced yellow bell peppers or decorate the perimeter of the plate with tangerine sections.

1. Place the shrimp, ginger, sesame oil, and cooking wine in a blender, and blend into a paste. Transfer to a bowl. Add the cornstarch, pepper, and sesame shake, and mix thoroughly.

2. Using a spoon or melon baller, shape the mixture into tablespoon-sized balls. Place the balls on a plate and steam for 5 to 7 minutes. Let cool.

3. Scoop watermelon and honeydew into tablespoon-sized balls.

4. Arrange a layer of honeydew balls on a serving plate. Place a layer of watermelon balls next, and top with a layer of shrimp balls. Serve.

NUTRITIONAL FACTS (PER APPETIZER)

Calories: 33 Carbohydrates: 1.9 g Cholesterol: 35 mg
Fat: 0.6 g Fiber: 0.1 g Protein: 4.7 g Sodium: 38 mg

Scallops with Orange Peel

Did you know that traditional Chinese doctors use orange peels to help cure coughs, calm queasy stomachs, and clear congested lungs? Although you can use dried orange peel in this recipe, try to use the fresh, which is much more flavorful.

1. To make the marinade, combine the cornstarch and water in a bowl, then mix in the remaining marinade ingredients. Add the scallops, toss to coat, and marinate in the refrigerator 30 minutes.

2. Lightly coat a nonstick wok or frying pan with cooking spray and place over medium heat. Reserving the marinade, add the scallops to the pan and sauté until they are white in color (about 2 minutes).

3. Add the water chestnuts and orange peel, mix with the scallops, and cook for 3 minutes.

4. Add the reserved marinade, and heat through.

5. Transfer to a serving bowl, top with green onion, and serve hot.

NUTRITIONAL FACTS (PER SERVING)

Calories: 158 Carbohydrates: 21.7 g Cholesterol: 25 mg
Fat: 0.9 g Fiber: 0.7 g Protein: 13.9 g Sodium: 155 mg

Yield: *6 servings*

1 pound medium scallops

16-ounce can water chestnuts, drained

1 teaspoon minced fresh orange peel

1 green onion, chopped

MARINADE

1 teaspoon cornstarch

2 tablespoons orange juice

2 teaspoons low-sodium soy sauce

1/2 teaspoon rice vinegar

4 cloves garlic, minced

2 teaspoons minced fresh ginger

1/2 teaspoon chili pepper flakes

1/2 teaspoon ground white pepper

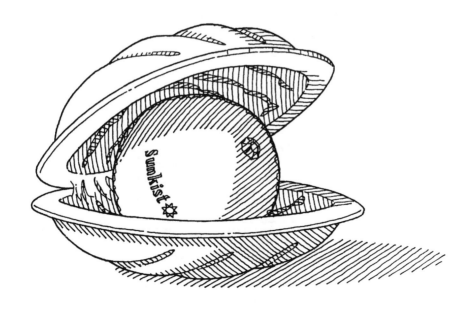

Party Rolls

Yield: 24 rolls
(15 cabbage, 9 salmon)

4 ounces smoked Atlantic salmon,
cut into 9 thin slices

15 large Napa cabbage leaves

1/4 cup thinly sliced red bell pepper

FILLING*

8 ounces fat-free cream cheese

2 tablespoons fat-free yogurt

3 sprigs cilantro, minced

*Instead of cheese filling, use a sweet-rice filling. Simply mix a cup of cooked sweet rice with 1 teaspoon rice vinegar and 1/2 teaspoon white pepper.

1. Place the cabbage leaves in boiling water until soft (4 to 5 minutes). Drain and cut into approximately 3-x-5-inch pieces.

2. Mix the filling ingredients together in a medium bowl.

3. Lay out the salmon slices and cabbage leaves on a clean, flat surface. Place 1 heaping teaspoon of filling in the center of each. Fold the right and left sides over the filling, then roll them up.

4. Arrange the salmon and cabbage rolls artistically on a serving plate. Decorate with bell pepper slices.

NUTRITIONAL FACTS (PER CABBAGE ROLL)

Calories: 17 Carbohydrates: 1.1 g Cholesterol: 3 mg
Fat: 0 g Fiber: 0.2 g Protein: 2.5 g Sodium: 93 mg

NUTRITIONAL FACTS (PER SALMON ROLL)

Calories: 46 Carbohydrates: 1.3 g Cholesterol: 11 mg
Fat: 1.3 g Fiber: 0.1 g Protein: 6.1 g Sodium: 161 mg

Scallops with Fruit Balls

Yield: 4 servings

8 ounces small scallops

2 mangos

4 ounces seedless watermelon

4 ounces honeydew melon

MARINADE

2 tablespoons fresh lemon juice

1/2 teaspoon ground white pepper

1/4 teaspoon five-spice powder

1. Combine the marinade ingredients in a bowl. Add the scallops, toss to coat, and marinate in the refrigerator for 15 minutes.

2. Using a spoon or melon baller, carve the mangos, watermelon, and honeydew into balls.

3. Add the fruit to a pot of boiling water and blanch (about 1 minute). Remove the fruit and drain.

4. Lightly coat a nonstick wok or frying pan with cooking spray and place over medium heat. Add the scallops and sauté until they are no longer translucent (3 to 5 minutes).

5. Add the fruit and gently mix with the scallops. Serve warm.

NUTRITIONAL FACTS (PER SERVING)

Calories: 141 Carbohydrates: 24.4 g Cholesterol: 18 mg
Fat: 1 g Fiber: 2.4 g Protein: 10.5 g Sodium: 96 mg

Clam Cake

1. Preheat the oven to 425°F.

2. Lightly coat a nonstick frying pan with cooking spray and place over medium heat. Add the ginger and sauté until it begins to brown. (2 to 3 minutes). Add the clams and continue to sauté another minute. Stir in the five-spice powder and cook 1 more minute.

3. Add the sweet rice and lemon juice to the clams and mix together thoroughly to form the filling.

4. Evenly divide the filling into thirds and spread on three of the tortillas. Sprinkle cilantro and green onion on each, top with another tortilla shell, and place the three "cakes" on a baking sheet.

5. Bake until the tortillas begin to crisp (10 to 12 minutes). Remove from the oven and allow to cool about 5 minutes.

6. Using a serrated knife, cut the tortillas in quarters, and transfer the wedges to a platter. Decorate with colorful fruit or vegetables and serve.

Yield: 12 servings

6 white flour tortillas (10-inch)

1 cup cooked sweet rice (warm)

1/4 cup minced clams

2 tablespoons minced fresh ginger

1/2 teaspoon five-spice powder

2 teaspoons fresh lemon juice

4 sprigs cilantro, chopped

3 green onions, minced

NUTRITIONAL FACTS (PER WEDGE)
Calories: 63 Carbohydrates: 12.8 g Cholesterol: 1 mg
Fat: 0.6 g Fiber: 2.3 g Protein: 2 g Sodium: 148 mg

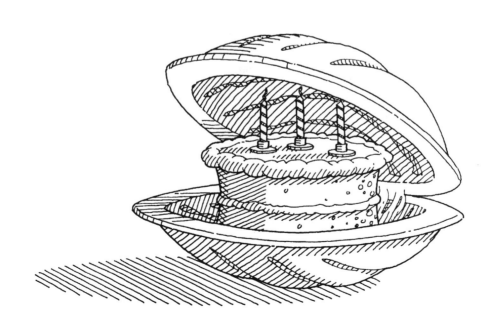

Trout with Szechuan Sauce

Yield: 6 servings

2 fresh whole rainbow trout (1 pound each), cleaned and scaled

3 cups frozen corn kernels

3 sprigs fresh cilantro, chopped

SAUCE

1 cup cold water

2 tablespoons cornstarch

2 tablespoons rice wine

2 tablespoons low-sodium soy sauce

1 tablespoon fresh lemon juice

1 tablespoon minced fresh ginger

$1/2$ teaspoon Mrs. Dash extra-spicy seasoning

$1/4$ teaspoon chili pepper flakes

1. To make the sauce, combine the cornstarch and water in a small bowl, then mix in the remaining sauce ingredients. Set aside.

2. Cut 3 to 4 quarter-inch-deep diagonal slashes along both sides of each fish.

3. Lightly coat a nonstick frying pan with cooking spray and place over medium heat. Add the fish, coat the tops with a little cooking spray, and cook until the skin starts to brown (3 to 4 minutes). Turn the fish over and cook the other side.

4. Add the corn and sauce. Reduce the heat to medium-low, and cook 2 to 3 minutes. Turn the fish and continue to cook until most of the sauce is absorbed. (If the sauce gets too thick, add another $1/4$-cup water.)

5. Remove the fish to a platter, top with cilantro, and serve.

NUTRITIONAL FACTS (PER SERVING)

Calories: 204 Carbohydrates: 19.8 g Cholesterol: 50 mg
Fat: 3.9 g Fiber: 2 g Protein: 19.5 g Sodium: 123 mg

Honan-Style Chinese Cooking

China's Yellow River runs through the Honan province, which is located in the southeast-central part of the country. Honan is famous for its fresh-water fish dishes, many of which are richly seasoned and spicy, while others are characteristically sweet-and-sour. Honan is most famous for its Yellow-River carp, which is well-known throughout China.

For a taste of delicious, low-fat Honan-style dishes, be sure to try the Crispy Trout on page 127, the Hot-and-Sour Cabbage on page 96, and the Spicy Tofu with Green Peas on page 84.

Crispy Trout

This is one of my husband's favorite dishes. It was one of the first things I cooked for him before we married. After several years together, I sometimes wonder if he married me for this dish! (There may be a bit of truth to the old adage that the way to a man's heart is through his stomach.) If you like things a bit spicier, add ¹/2 teaspoon of Mrs. Dash extra-spicy seasoning to the ingredient list.

Yield: *5 servings*

2-pound whole trout, cleaned and scaled

2 tablespoons grated ginger

2 tablespoons cooking wine

¹/2 teaspoon five-spice powder

1 teaspoon black pepper

1 teaspoon Mrs. Dash seasoning

2 green onions, coarsely chopped

2 sprigs cilantro, coarsely chopped

1. Cut 3 to 4 quarter-inch-deep diagonal slashes along both sides of the fish.

2. Briskly rub the wine, five-spice powder, and Mrs. Dash seasoning on the sides and inside the cleaned fish.

3. Fill the slashes and the insides of the fish with ginger, green onion, and cilantro.

4. Place the fish in a nonstick baking dish that has been lightly coated with cooking spray. Add a little spray to the top of the fish and place in the broiler on a low rack. Cook the fish until the skin begins to brown (10 to 15 minutes). Remove the fish from the broiler, turn it over, and spray the other side with a little cooking spray (never use the spray near the flames of a broiler).

5. Return the fish to the broiler and cook until the skin is brown and the flesh easily flakes with a fork (another 10 minutes).

6. Serve hot with fresh vegetables.

NUTRITIONAL FACTS (PER SERVING)
Calories: 115 Carbohydrates: 0.8 g Cholesterol: 52 mg
Fat: 3.1 g Fiber: 0.3 g Protein: 18.2 g Sodium: 58 mg

9. Dessert Delights

Unlike many Americans, who look forward to a sweet dessert at the end of a meal, the Chinese usually end their meals with fresh fruit, which serves to cleanse the palate. Traditionally, in China, desserts are served only on festive occasions when family and friends gather together. Occasionally, dessert treats are also enjoyed between meals, usually with a cup of tea (*see* Tea Time on page 130). Not only are desserts eaten less frequently in China they contain much less sugar and fat than their American counterparts.

In this chapter, I present delicious low-fat desserts that are decidedly Chinese, and probably different from most desserts you have ever tried. Be sure to try the delicately sweet Full Moon Dumplings on a cold winter's day, or enjoy a crisp Almond Cookie along with a soothing cup of tea. And don't forget the luscious fruit shakes—they're great!

After trying these tasty treats, I'm confident you will agree that desserts do not have to be high in fat or loaded with sugar to be delicious.

Tea Time

Although many countries have grown tea for centuries, there are only three basic tea types: black, red, and green. Black tea is made from fully fermented leaves. It yields an amber-colored, full-bodied tea without bitterness. Internationally, most commercial teas consist of black-tea varieties; orange pekoe and pekoe are the most notable. Red tea is semifermented and comes from a Chinese tea plant known as chesima; it has a subtle, slightly bitter taste. Green tea is the tea of choice in China, Japan, and Taiwan. Its unfermented leaves yield a mild, slightly bitter, pale green liquid. To enrich green tea's fragrance, sometimes certain flowers—jasmine, orange buds, and chrysanthemums—are added. Recently, green tea has gained attention because of its possible health benefits—studies have indicated it is a fat-burning cancer preventive.

For centuries, the Chinese have used cold, clear-flowing stream water to brew tea. (Years ago, a jug of fresh, clean water accompanied by a poem was a common gift.) Today, always use fresh bottled spring water for brewing tea. Never use tap water, which contains chemicals and can alter the taste of the brew.

Although there are many methods for brewing tea, I have found steeping the leaves in a teapot to be the best. The pot should be made of china, glass, or stainless steel, not plastic or aluminum. (And never use an aluminum kettle for boiling the brewing water either.) Always preheat the teapot by filling it with hot water while the brewing water is heating up in another pot.

When boiling the brewing water, note that different teas require different water temperatures. For green teas, steep the leaves in water that has just begun to boil. Red tea leaves are best steeped in boiling water that is bubbling gently and steaming. For black teas, use water that has come to a full rolling boil.

When the brewing water is ready, pour out the hot water that has been preheating the teapot. Add the proper amount of tea to the pot—one teabag or one heaping teaspoon per cup of boiling water. Add the boiling water, cover, and steep for three to five minutes. The flavor increases the longer the leaves steep.

Preheat the teacups with hot water as you did the teapot. When the tea is ready, pour out the hot water from the teacups and pour in the fresh-brewed tea.

A wise old Chinese man wrote what he thought were the "proper moments" for drinking tea:

- When one's heart and hands are idle.
- When engaged in conversation with charming friends and slender concubines.
- In a pavilion overlooking lotus flowers on a summer day.
- When tired after reading poetry.
- When a feast is over and the guests have gone.

From this inspiration, I have come up with my own modern-day tea moments:

- During relaxed conversations with friends.
- Under the light of a full moon.
- On a cold snowy winter morning after a good night's sleep.
- Late at night while planning the next day's events with your partner.
- At the end of a feast while your spouse is cleaning up.
- After balancing your checkbook.

One thing is certain, there is no right or wrong time to enjoy a cup of tea. For centuries, it has been a beverage associated with relaxation, peace, and friendship. What are your favorite tea times?

Almond Gel with Mixed Fruits

The agar-agar called for in this recipe is a sea-vegetable product that is commonly used to make molded vegetable aspics and gelatin-like desserts Containing no fat or calories, agar-agar is sold in most health food stores and Asian markets.

Yield: *6 servings*

1. Soak the agar-agar according to package instructions.

2. In a medium pot, bring the soaked agar-agar to a boil, reduce the heat to medium-low, and cook until it is dissolved (2 to 3 minutes).

3. Stir in the sugar, Rice Dream, and almond extract. Remove from the heat and mix thoroughly.

4. Pour the mixture into a 10- or 12-inch pan and refrigerate until set (about 2 hours).

5. Cut the gel into bite-sized cubes, top with melon and cherries, and serve.

.4 ounces (11 grams) agar-agar

5 cups water

1/2 cup sugar

1/2 cup Rice Dream beverage, or reduced-fat soymilk

1 tablespoon almond extract

1 cup diced fresh melon and cherries

NUTRITIONAL FACTS (PER SERVING)

Calories: 42.3 Carbohydrates: 10.4 g Cholesterol: 0 mg
Fat: 0.1 g Fiber: 0.4 g Protein: 0.2 g Sodium: 8 mg

Almond Cookies

Yield: 36 cookies

2 cups unbleached white flour

½ teaspoon baking soda

6 tablespoons reduced-fat margarine

1 cup sugar

1 teaspoon almond extract

3 tablespoons egg substitute

36 blanched almond halves

1. Preheat the oven to 300°F. Lightly coat a nonstick baking sheet with cooking spray and set aside.

2. Combine the flour and baking powder together in a bowl and set aside.

3. Using a hand mixer, beat together the margarine, sugar, and almond extract until well-combined (about 5 minutes). Gradually add the egg substitute to form a smooth mixture.

4. Add the flour, a little at a time, to the mixture. Stir well to form a stiff dough.

5. Drop slightly rounded teaspoons of the dough onto the baking sheet about 2 inches apart. Press an almond half on the center of each, flattening the dough slightly.

6. Bake the cookies until golden brown (15 to 20 minutes). Cool the cookies on the pan for 1 minute, then transfer them to a wire rack to cool completely. Serve immediately or store in an airtight container.

NUTRITIONAL FACTS (PER COOKIE)

Calories: 54 Carbohydrates: 10.6 g Cholesterol: 0 mg
Fat: 1 g Fiber: 0 g Protein: 0.9 g Sodium: 36 mg

Top: Baked Sole with Tomatoes (page 118)
Right: Simple Rice (page 61)
Bottom Left: Tofu-Stuffed Green Peppers
(page 87)

Left: Baked Lemon Pudding (page 136)
Bottom Right: Almond Cookies (page 132)

Full Moon Dumplings

Yield: *16 dumplings*

Also called Tang Yuan, these sweet-tasting rice-flour dumplings are traditionally eaten during the Chinese Lantern Festival (see page 86).

2 cups sweet rice flour

1 cup cold water

1 cup red bean paste

1 teaspoon sesame seeds

1. Mix the bean paste and sesame seeds together in a small bowl and set aside.

2. Combine the rice flour and water to form a smooth dough. Place the dough on a lightly floured surface and shape it into a 14-inch roll. Evenly divide the roll into 16 pieces.

3. Using the palm of your hand, flatten the pieces of dough into 2-inch circles. Place $^1/_2$ teaspoon of red bean paste in the center of each circle. Gather the edges around the filling and gently roll each circle into a ball-shaped dumpling. Place the dumplings on a lightly floured plate.

4. Bring 6 cups of water to boil in a large pot. Drop the dumplings, one at a time, into the boiling water. Cook over medium heat until the dumplings rise to the surface and become translucent (about 5 minutes). Remove the dumplings with a slotted spoon.

5. Serve hot in a little of the cooking broth.

NUTRITIONAL FACTS (PER DUMPLING)
Calories: 129 Carbohydrates: 27.4 g Cholesterol: 0 mg
Fat: 0.9 g Fiber: 0.5 g Protein: 2.3 g Sodium: 74 mg

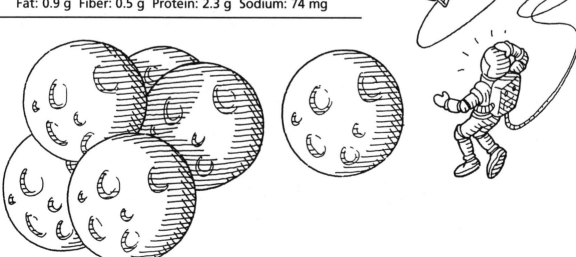

Pear-Lemon-Ginger Shake

Yield: *5 servings*

8 medium-sized ripe pears

½ cup fresh lemon juice

1 teaspoon minced fresh ginger

6 ice cubes

1. Peel, core, and cube the pears.

2. Place all of the ingredients in a blender. Blend at high speed until smooth and frosty.

3. Pour into glasses and serve immediately for best color and taste.

NUTRITIONAL FACTS (PER 8-OUNCE SERVING)

Calories: 163 Carbohydrates: 41.7 g Cholesterol: 0 mg
Fat: 1.2 g Fiber: 6.9 g Protein: 1.2 g Sodium: 5 mg

Melon-Lemon-Ginger Shake

Yield: *5 servings*

2 cups cantaloupe cubes

2 cups honeydew cubes

¼ cup fresh lemon juice

½ teaspoon minced fresh ginger

5 ice cubes

1. Place all of the ingredients in a blender. Blend at high speed until smooth and frosty.

2. Pour into glasses and serve immediately for best color and taste.

NUTRITIONAL FACTS (PER 8-OUNCE SERVING)

Calories: 50 Carbohydrates: 12.7 g Cholesterol: 0 mg
Fat: 0.2 g Fiber: 1 g Protein: 1 g Sodium: 13 mg

Banana Shake

1. Peel the bananas and cut them into pieces.

2. Place all of the ingredients, except the ice cubes, in a blender. Blend on high until smooth. Add the ice cubes and continue to blend until smooth and frosty.

3. Pour into glasses and serve immediately for best color and taste.

Yield: 5 servings

2 ripe bananas

2 cups Rice Dream beverage, or reduced-fat soymilk

1 cup white grape juice

¼ cup instant oatmeal

1½ teaspoons sesame seeds

5 ice cubes

NUTRITIONAL FACTS (PER 8-OUNCE SERVING)

Calories: 142 Carbohydrates: 31.5 g Cholesterol: 0 mg
Fat: 1.7 g Fiber: 1.2 g Protein: 1.7 g Sodium: 41 mg

Cool Summer Mango Shake

1. Peel, seed, and cube the mangos. Peel and section the oranges, remove the seeds, then cut the sections in half.

2. Place the ice cubes in a blender and blend at medium speed for 1 minute. Add the mango and oranges, and blend at high speed until smooth and frosty.

3. Pour into glasses, garnish with mint leaves, and serve immediately for best color and taste.

Yield: 5 servings

2 large mangos

8 medium oranges

10 ice cubes

4 fresh mint leaves

NUTRITIONAL FACTS (PER 8-OUNCE SERVING)

Calories: 149 Carbohydrates: 37.1 g Cholesterol: 0 mg
Fat: 0.9 g Fiber: 2.6 g Protein: 2.5 g Sodium: 2 mg

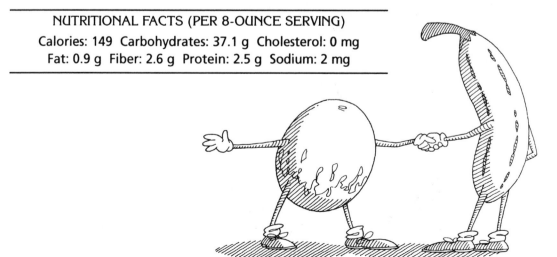

Baked Lemon Pudding

Yield: 6 servings

16 ounces soft low-fat tofu

1½ cups whole-wheat bread cubes

3 tablespoons egg substitute

⅓ cup fresh lemon juice

½ cup Rice Dream beverage, or reduced-fat soymilk

½ cup sugar

¼ cup minced dried pineapple

2 tablespoons grated lemon or orange peel

1. Preheat the oven to 350°F. Lightly coat a 9-inch-square baking dish with Baker's Joy cooking spray and set aside.

2. Using a spoon, mash the tofu in a bowl. Add the egg substitute, lemon juice, Rice Dream, sugar, and pineapple, and blend thoroughly. Gently stir in the bread cubes.

3. Spread the pudding mixture evenly in the baking dish and sprinkle with lemon peel. Bake until the top turns golden brown (20 to 25 minutes).

4. Spoon into individual serving bowls and serve hot.

NUTRITIONAL FACTS (PER 1-CUP SERVING)

Calories: 106 Carbohydrates: 20.1 g Cholesterol: 0 mg
Fat: 1.7 g Fiber: 1.5 g Protein: 3.8 g Sodium: 60 mg

Coconut Fruit Gel

If you cannot find coconut gelatin, which is sold in most Asian markets, use unflavored gelatin and a teaspoon or two of coconut flavoring instead.

Yield: *6 servings*

7-ounce package coconut gelatin

5 cups Rice Dream beverage, or reduced-fat soymilk

1 cup bite-sized pineapple cubes*

* If using canned pineapple, be sure to drain it.

1. Combine the gelatin and Rice Dream in a medium pan and bring to a boil. Pour the mixture into a 10- or 12-inch pan.

2. Allow the mixture to cool, then gently mix in the pineapple. Refrigerate until set (about 2 hours).

3. Cut the gelatin into squares and serve.

NUTRITIONAL FACTS (PER SERVING)
Calories: 137 Carbohydrates: 29.9 g Cholesterol: 0 mg
Fat: 1.8 g Fiber: 0.3 g Protein: 1.6 g Sodium: 75 mg

Red Bean and Sago Soup

This sweet soup is traditionally served at the end of a meal or as a snack. The sweet red bean paste and the sago (a type of starch) is sold at health food stores and Asian markets.

Yield: *10 servings*

8 ounces red bean paste

1/2 cup sago

1/4 cup grated orange peel

1 cup sugar

8 cups water

1 teaspoon toasted sesame seeds

1. Soften the sago by soaking it in 2 cups of water for 15 minutes.

2. In a large pot, combine the softened sago, bean paste, orange peel, sugar, and water. Bring to a boil, reduce the heat to low, and simmer for 40 minutes.

3. Sprinkle with sesame seeds and serve.

NUTRITIONAL FACTS (PER 1-CUP SERVING)
Calories: 184 Carbohydrates: 44.1 g Cholesterol: 0 mg
Fat: 0.9 g Fiber: 0.1 g Protein: 0.7 g Sodium: 1 mg

Nin Go

Yield: *10 slices*

1 cup sugar

2 cups water

2½ cups glutinous rice flour

½ cup raisins

½ cup chopped dates, cherries,
   or other fruit

In China, the traditional New Year's meal ends with this sweet cake. It is believed that those who eat Nin Go will experience good fortune in the year ahead. For more information on the Chinese New Year, see page 43.

1. Stir the sugar and water together in a large mixing bowl. Add the flour, about a cup at a time, and mix to form a smooth batter. Stir in the raisins and dates.

2. Coat a 10-inch round cake pan with Baker's Joy cooking spray, then pour in the batter.

3. Place the cake pan on a steamer basket that has been set over boiling water. Steam for 40 to 50 minutes, or until the Nin Go has risen and becomes translucent.

4. Allow the cake to cool, then cut it into wedges and serve.

NUTRITIONAL FACTS (PER SLICE)
Calories: 271 Carbohydrates: 64.7 g Cholesterol: 0 mg
Fat: 0.6 g Fiber: 2.2 g Protein: 2.7 g Sodium: 3 mg

Fortune Cookies

Did you know that the sweet, crisp fortune cookie, complete with its fun-spirited message, is an American creation?

Yield: 25 cookies

1. Cut 25 strips of white paper, about 2-x-³/4-inches. Write a fortune on each strip.

2. In a large bowl, combine the flour and baking powder. Set aside.

3. Cream together the margarine and sugar. Add the egg and vanilla and beat until smooth. Add the flour mixture, a little at a time, until a dough forms. Gather the dough into a ball.

4. Lightly flour a clean work surface. Roll out half the dough until it is very thin. With a circular cookie cutter or the top of a glass (about 3¹/2 inches across), cut out circles of dough.

5. Place a fortune on the top half of each circle, then fold the bottom half over the fortune to form a half circle. Pinch the edges to seal. Bring the ends of the half moon together until they are almost touching (see figure below).

6. Place the cookies on an unoiled baking sheet and place in a preheated 425° F oven. Bake for about 10 minutes, or until the cookies are light brown. Allow to cool before serving.

3¹/4 cups unbleached white flour

¹/2 teaspoon baking powder

1 cup reduced-fat margarine, softened

¹/2 cup sugar

¹/4 cup egg substitute

2¹/2 teaspoons vanilla extract

NUTRITIONAL FACTS (PER SLICE)
Calories: 82 Carbohydrates: 15.4 g Cholesterol: 0 mg
Fat: 1.5 g Fiber: 0 g Protein: 1.6 g Sodium: 79 mg

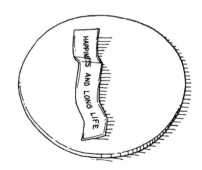

a. Cut out circles of dough.

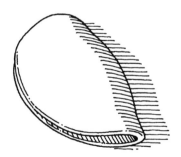

b. Fold the dough in half enclosing the fortune.

c. Bring the ends together until they are almost touching.

Forming a Fortune Cookie

Resource List

The ingredients called for in this book can be found in most supermarkets, health foods stores, and Asian markets. If, however, you are unable to find a particular item, the following list should guide you to a manufacturer who can either sell the desired product to you directly or inform you of the nearest retail store.

Alberto-Culver Company
2525 Armitage Avenue
Melrose Park, IL 60160
(800) 622-3274
Mrs. Dash seasoning blends.

Arrowhead Mills, Inc.
PO Box 2059
Hereford, TX 79045
(800) 749-0730
Easy-Spreading Peanut Butter.

China Bowl Trading Company, Inc.
PO Box 454
Westport, CT 06881
(203) 222-0381
Rice noodles; chili paste.

China Dragon Gourmet Enterprises
1714 Topaz Drive
Loveland, CO 80537
(970) 669-7666
Low-sodium soy sauce.

Denver Tofu Company
3825 Blake Street
Denver, CO 80205
(303) 295-6848
Fresh spring roll and dumpling wrappers.

Dynasty
PO Box 7251
San Francisco, CA 94120
(415) 871-1660
Mustard sauce varieties.

East-West Specialty Sauces, Inc.
2045 South Valentia
Denver, CO 80222
(303) 695-6369
Low-sodium teriyaki sauce varieties.

Eden Foods, Inc.
701 Tecumseh Road
Clinton, MI 49236
(313) 973-9400
Sesame shakes.

Huy Fong Foods, Inc.
5001 Earle Avenue
Rosemead, CA 91770
(818) 286-8328
Chili paste.

Imagine Foods, Inc.
350 Cambridge Avenue, Suite 350
Palo Alto, CA 94306
(415) 327-1444
Rice Dream beverage.

Morinaga Nutritional Foods, Inc.
2050 West 190th Street, Suite 110
Torrance, CA 90504
(800) NOW-TOFU
Mori-Nu low-fat tofu varieties.

Rice Road c/o MCC Foods American, Inc.
1300 East 223 Street, Suite 412
Carson, CA 90745
(800) 959-3912
Honey mustard, low-sodium teriyaki sauce.

Vitasoy
400 Oyster Point Boulevard, #201
South San Francisco, CA 94080
(415) 583-9888 (800) 848-2709
Fresh spring roll and dumpling wrappers.

Westbrae Naturals
1065 East Walnut Street
Carson, CA 90746
(310) 886-8200 (800) 776-1276
Low-sodium miso paste.

Metric Conversions

Conversion Table		
LIQUID		
When You Know	**Multiply By**	**To Determine**
teaspoons	5.0	milliliters
tablespoons	15.0	milliliters
fluid ounces	30.0	milliliters
cups	0.24	liters
pints	0.47	liters
quarts	0.95	liters
WEIGHT		
When You Know	**Multiply By**	**To Determine**
ounces	28.0	grams
pounds	0.45	kilograms

Common Liquid Conversions

Measurement	=	Liters
1/4 cup	=	0.06 liters
1/2 cup	=	0.12 liters
3/4 cup	=	0.18 liters
1 cup	=	0.24 liters
1 1/4 cups	=	0.30 liters
1 1/2 cups	=	0.36 liters
2 cups	=	0.48 liters
2 1/2 cups	=	0.60 liters
3 cups	=	0.72 liters
3 1/2 cups	=	0.84 liters
4 cups	=	0.96 liters
4 1/2 cups	=	1.08 liters
5 cups	=	1.20 liters
5 1/2 cups	=	1.32 liters

Measurement	=	Milliliters
1/4 teaspoon	=	1.25 milliliters
1/2 teaspoon	=	2.50 milliliters
3/4 teaspoon	=	3.75 milliliters
1 teaspoon	=	5.00 milliliters
1 1/4 teaspoons	=	6.25 milliliters
1 1/2 teaspoons	=	7.50 milliliters
1 3/4 teaspoons	=	8.75 milliliters
2 teaspoons	=	10.0 milliliters
1 tablespoon	=	15.0 milliliters
2 tablespoons	=	30.0 milliliters

Converting Fahrenheit to Celsius

Fahrenheit	=	Celsius
200—205	=	95
220—225	=	105
245—250	=	120
275	=	135
300—305	=	150
325—330	=	165
345—350	=	175
370—375	=	190
400—405	=	205
425—430	=	220
445—450	=	230
470—475	=	245
500	=	260

Index

C

W